# Quilt
# Revival

### Updated Patterns from the '30s

## Nancy Mahoney

### Martingale®
& COMPANY

Quilt Revival: Updated Patterns from the '30s
© 2006 by Nancy Mahoney

That Patchwork Place® is an imprint of
Martingale & Company®.

Martingale & Company
20205 144th Avenue NE
Woodinville, WA 98072-8478 USA
www.martingale-pub.com

## Credits

President • Nancy J. Martin
CEO • Daniel J. Martin
VP and General Manager • Tom Wierzbicki
Publisher • Jane Hamada
Editorial Director • Mary V. Green
Managing Editor • Tina Cook
Technical Editor • Darra Williamson
Copy Editor • Ellen Balstad
Design Director • Stan Green
Illustrator • Robin Strobel
Cover and Text Designer • Shelly Garrison
Photographer • Brent Kane

Printed in China
11 10 09 08 07 06        8 7 6 5 4 3 2 1

**Library of Congress Cataloging-in-Publication Data**
Mahoney, Nancy.
    Quilt revival : updated patterns from the '30s /
    Nancy Mahoney.
        p. cm.
    ISBN 1-56477-643-3
    1. Quilting—Patterns. 2. Patchwork—Patterns.
    3. Quilts—United States—History—1933-1945.
    I. Title.
    TT835.M27154987 2006
    746.46'041—dc22
                                                    2005028411

## MISSION STATEMENT
Dedicated to providing quality products and service to inspire creativity.

## Dedication

To my maternal great-grandmother—Catherine Ellen Fowler Clark Carty; and to other quilters in the 1930s who learned how to be frugal with every scrap. Their quilts are the embodiment of the resourcefulness, day-to-day struggles, and triumphs of an entire generation of women.

## Acknowledgments

I'd like to extend a very special thanks to the following people and companies:

Dawn Kelly, machine quilter extraordinaire, who beautifully quilted many of the quilts in this book. On numerous occasions, she readily accepted "one more project" to help me meet my deadline;

Marcus Brothers, whose lovely fabrics enriched so many of the quilts;

American & Efird and Marci Brier for Mettler and Signature threads;

Hobbs Bonded Fibers and H. D. Wilbanks for batting;

The enthusiastic people at Martingale & Company. Without your many talents, there would be no book!

And most of all, Tom Reichert, who is always there to cheer me on!

# CONTENTS

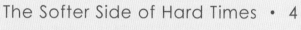

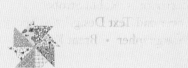

# THE *Softer Side* OF *Hard Times*

In the middle of the Roaring Twenties, as the United States celebrated its 150th birthday, a wave of nostalgia swept the nation. Quilts gained newfound popularity as emblems of a vanishing past. The happenstance of the Great Depression with the national quilt revival of the 1930s provided many with a creative way to "make something of nothing." In the midst of such uncertainty, the quilts stitched with bright, cheery fabrics warmed bodies and minds.

During the Great Depression, when money was scarce, quiltmaking became an outlet for self-expression. Although family and friends continued as sources for quilt patterns, women turned more and more frequently to current magazines and booklets for inspiration. Women also created new interpretations of traditional quilt designs by looking at photos from magazines. And some of the most striking designs were made for quilt competitions.

A Century of Progress International Exposition in Chicago in 1933 included a national quilt contest sponsored by Sears, Roebuck and Company, with a grand prize of $1000—a generous sum during the height of the Depression. That same year, the Mountain Mist quilt batting company held a three-day quilt exhibit in Detroit. Quilts exhibited at country fairs also met with increasing enthusiasm.

These quilt shows, and many others, touched off a demand for quilt patterns. Women began writing to magazines and newspapers for help in finding patterns. Publications, primarily in rural areas, responded to these requests and began printing pictures of quilt blocks accompanied by brief descriptions. Old patterns were often renamed, resulting in multiple names for the same block.

The *Kansas City Star*, the *San Antonio Light*, the *Houston Post*, and the *Journal* in Portland, Oregon, are just a few of the many newspapers that printed quilt block patterns. By 1934, approximately 400 metropolitan newspapers featured articles on quiltmaking, with the quilt article being the most popular Sunday feature. Many newspapers published syndicated columns under names such as Aunt Martha, Alice Brooks, or Laura Wheeler. Most newspapers printed one quilt pattern a week for at least ten years—a total of 520 quilt patterns! They published old patterns, variations of old patterns, original patterns, and variations of original patterns. While some of these patterns were almost unworkable, others provided inspiring new designs, including appliqué and animal motifs. The illustrations commonly showed the blocks made from the combination of many prints with solid colors. The Double Wedding Ring pattern was possibly the most well liked of the period. Other popular patterns included Dresden Plate, Sunbonnet Sue, and Grandmother's Flower Garden.

Enthusiastic quilters often clipped the patterns from the newspapers and pasted them in notebooks or composition books. Readers who wanted full-size patterns sent 10¢ or 15¢ to the local paper, which forwarded the request to a syndicate office. In return, the quilter received a block chart, carefully drawn pattern pieces, directions for the quilt, yardage charts, and illustrations of the quilt.

In the 1930s, women wanted quilts in what were considered modern pastels and cheerful color schemes. Specific colors are seen in almost every quilt from the '30s. Most of the quilts from this period were scrap-bag style; quilters combined all kinds of colors and prints, pulling them together with white or other solid colors.

Since the mid-1990s, fabric manufacturers have reproduced prints from the '30s due to their ever-increasing popularity. Many quilters love the clear, light, bright colors and have embraced these fabrics. The resulting quilts have a homey quality reminiscent of simpler times.

Many years ago, I was lucky to find two scrapbooks of quilt patterns collected during the '30s by women in different parts of the country. I selected a few of my favorite blocks from the scrapbooks, updated the patterns using quick and easy techniques, and used '30s reproduction fabrics to create the wonderful quilts in *Quilt Revival.*

Join with me in celebrating the cheerful fabrics and quilt designs of the '30s. You're sure to have fun making these cheerful quilts.

# LIGHT, SUNNY QUILTS

There are several characteristics that distinguish '30s quilts from those of other periods. The most distinctive aspect of quilts from this period is the fabric, which was intentionally designed to cheer the soul. In general, the print designs were simpler and less stylized than those from earlier periods. Many fabrics were printed in one or two colors on a white background. Large-scale floral prints became popular again. Geometric prints and cute animal prints were also popular themes.

Color is another outstanding feature; pastel or light, sunny color schemes are seen in most, if not all, quilts from the '30s. Some of the most common colors were a particular '30s green (also called Nile green), pink, lavender, buttery yellow, and light blue. Red, bluish green (or aqua), peach (and other members of the orange family), and soft brown or tan also appeared in quilts during the '30s. These colors were used over and over in prints—either as one color on white, or as several colors with white in a splashy design.

Blocks and fabrics from the '30s

The unique colors and styles of the '30s fabrics and quilts are still with us today. Many of our favorite quilts use a "scrap bag" of prints coordinated with a solid color or a subtle print that looks like a solid.

Most of the quilts in this book are scrappy and require small amounts of different fabrics. As you choose the fabrics for your quilt, remember to use a variety of prints that vary in scale and texture.

In the style of traditional '30s quilts, many of the projects use a cream solid to unify the design. Muslin, white, or other solid colors can also be used instead of cream.

Assorted blue prints

Assorted pink prints

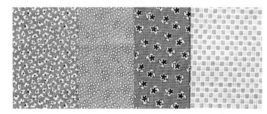

Assorted green prints

Assorted lavender prints

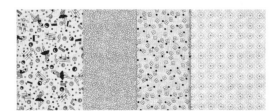

Assorted yellow prints

Assorted red prints

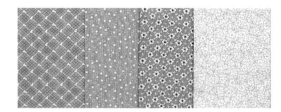

Assorted bluish green or aqua prints

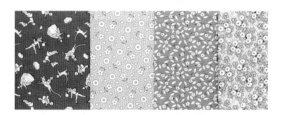

Assorted peach and orange prints

## BUILDING YOUR FABRIC STASH

Fat quarters (18" x 21") or fat eighths (9" x 21") are a great way to add fabrics to your stash. Look for these wonderful little bundles in baskets or bins at your local quilt store, in quilting catalogs, and on quilting Web sites. You can also purchase precut, prepackaged squares of a particular type of fabric—perfect for that scrappy-looking quilt!

# $\mathcal{Q}$UILTING $\mathcal{B}$ASICS

In the pages that follow, you'll find valuable information for the successful completion of your quilt. All the special techniques needed to complete your quilt are covered in these sections.

## ROTARY CUTTING

Instructions for rotary cutting are provided for all quilts, and *all rotary-cutting measurements include ¼"-wide seam allowances*. If you're unfamiliar with rotary cutting, refer to *The Quilter's Quick Reference Guide* by Candace Eisner Strick (Martingale & Company, 2004) for more detailed rotary-cutting instructions. Basic rotary-cutting tools include a rotary cutter, an 18" x 24" cutting mat, and a 6" x 24" acrylic ruler. You'll be able to make all the projects in this book with this size ruler, although I find a 6" Bias Square® very useful for making clean-up cuts as shown at right and for crosscutting squares and rectangles. Note that rotary-cutting instructions are written for right-handers; reverse the instructions if you are left-handed.

### *Cutting Strips*

It is essential that you cut strips at an exact right angle to the folded edge of your fabric. Rotary cutting squares, rectangles, and other shapes begins with cutting accurate strips.

Press the fabric, and then fold it in half with the selvages together. Place the fabric on your cutting mat with the folded edge nearest to your body. Align a Bias Square with the fold of the fabric and place a 6" x 24" ruler to the left so that the raw edges of the fabric are covered.

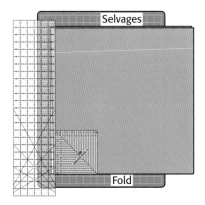

Remove the Bias Square and make a rotary cut along the right edge of the long ruler. Remove the long ruler and gently remove the waste strip. This is called a cleanup cut.

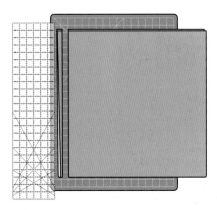

Align the desired strip width on the ruler with the cut edge of the fabric, and carefully cut a strip. After cutting three or four strips, realign the Bias Square along the fold and make a new cleanup cut if necessary.

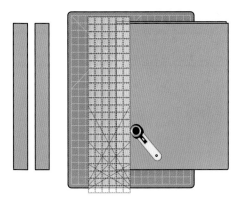

## *Cutting Squares and Rectangles*

To cut squares and rectangles, cut a strip in the desired width and carefully remove the selvage ends by making a cleanup cut. Align the desired measurements on the ruler (or Bias Square) with the left edge of the strip and cut a square or rectangle. Continue cutting until you have the required number of pieces.

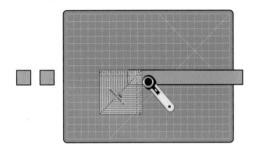

# MAKING UNITS FROM STRIP SETS

You can make multiple units more accurately and efficiently if you sew strips into strip sets and then crosscut them into segments. By using a rotary cutter, you can cut many pieces at the same time and often eliminate the use of templates. The following steps describe how to make strip sets for a four-patch unit; use the same process for constructing other strip sets and units.

❶ Cut the specific number of strips in the required width for the quilt you are making. Arrange the strips in the correct color combinations. With right sides together, sew the strips together along the long edges. Press the seams toward the darker fabric unless instructed otherwise.

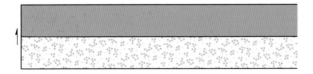

❷ Place one strip set on top of another strip set, right sides together, with the light fabric on top of the dark fabric.

❸ Make a cleanup cut to trim the ends of the strip sets. Then cut the strip sets into segments. The segment width is specified in the directions for each quilt.

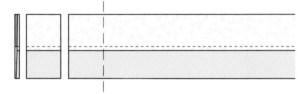

❹ Stitch the segment pairs together using a ¼"-wide seam allowance.

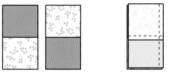

Four-patch unit

## TECHNIQUE TIP

When pressing long seams, first press the seam flat from the wrong side to smooth out any puckers. Be sure to use an up-and-down motion rather than the back-and-forth, gliding motion typical of ironing, to avoid stretching the fabric. Open the sewn unit and, from the right side, press in the direction indicated in the project diagram. Use the tip of the iron to gently push the fabric over the seam.

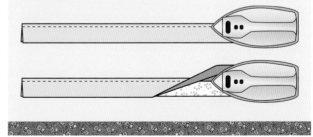

# HALF-SQUARE-TRIANGLE UNITS

Many of the quilts in this book include half-square-triangle units; that is, two half-square triangles sewn together along their long edges to make a square. I make these units the easy way, without cutting triangles.

**Note: Pressing the unit is the final step, so take extra care not to distort the half-square-triangle unit while pressing.**

**1** Cut two squares, one of each fabric, to the size specified in the cutting list. (This measurement equals the finished short side of the triangle plus ⅞".)

**2** Use a sharp pencil and a ruler to draw a diagonal line from corner to corner on the wrong side of the lighter square. Layer the two squares right sides together with the marked square on top and raw edges aligned. Sew ¼" on each side of the drawn diagonal line.

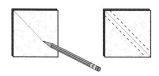

**3** Cut on the drawn line with a rotary cutter and ruler. Press the seams toward the darker fabric unless instructed otherwise. Trim the dog-ears (the little triangles that stick out at the corners). Each pair of squares will yield two half-square-triangle units.

## TECHNIQUE TIP

If the presser foot on your sewing machine measures exactly ¼" from the center of the needle to the edge of the presser foot, you can align the edge of the presser foot with the marked diagonal line to achieve a perfect ¼" seam allowance. Otherwise, after drawing a diagonal line from corner to corner, draw a line ¼" on either side of the center diagonal line. Stitch on these lines, and then cut along the centerline.

 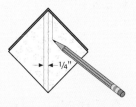

# CUT CORNERS

Several of the quilts in this book feature blocks made with the cut-corner technique. This is a simple way to create triangle shapes without actually cutting triangles or sewing on a bias-cut edge. This technique uses only squares and rectangles.

**1** Cut squares the size specified in the cutting list. Draw a diagonal line from corner to corner on the wrong side of the squares as directed.

**2** With right sides together, position the squares on the larger square or rectangle as directed in the quilt instructions. Sew *directly on* the drawn line.

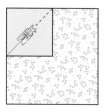

**3** Trim away the excess fabric, leaving a ¼"-wide seam allowance. Press the seams toward the corner triangle.

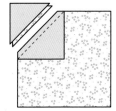 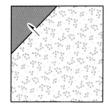

# PRESSING

Pressing is one of the keys to precise piecing. It is important to carefully press your work after stitching each seam. Set your iron on the cotton setting and use a padded pressing surface to prevent the seam allowances from creating ridges on the right side of the pieced unit. Use a pressing cloth between the iron and the pieced unit when ironing areas with multiple seams. (This protects your fabrics from becoming glazed and shiny under the iron.) To avoid possible distortion, allow the pieces to cool before moving them from the pressing surface.

In most situations, seams are pressed to one side, usually toward the darker fabric. When sewing one unit to another unit, press seams that need to match in opposite directions. The two opposing seams will "lock" in place and evenly distribute the fabric bulk.

Pressing arrows are included in the project illustrations when it is necessary to press the seams in a specific direction. Following these arrows will help in constructing the blocks and assembling the quilt top. When no arrows are shown, you will frequently find instruction in the text to guide you. If neither diagrams nor text indicate a preferred direction, you can press the seams in either direction. In general, it is common to press seams toward the darker fabric or toward the section with fewer seams.

## TECHNIQUE TIP

The following technique can be useful when joining four fabric pieces or units. Try it to create opposing seams and reduce bulk where four seams come together.

After the seam is sewn, use a seam ripper to remove one or two stitches from the seam allowance as shown. Gently reposition the seam allowances to evenly distribute the fabric. Press the seams in opposite directions.

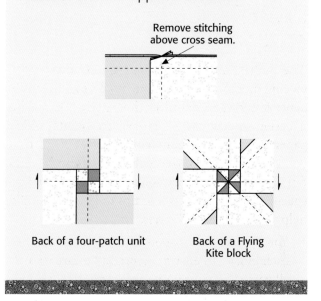

Remove stitching above cross seam.

Back of a four-patch unit

Back of a Flying Kite block

# MACHINE-PIECING TEMPLATES

The Quilt without a Name block used in the quilt "Chinese Checkers" on page 52 has odd-shaped fabric pieces that must be cut using piecing templates. To make templates, trace the patterns provided onto template plastic with a fine-tipped, permanent-ink pen, making sure to trace the lines exactly. On the right side of the template, mark the fabric grain line as shown on the pattern. All template patterns include seam allowances. For future reference, you may also want to write the block or quilt name and piece letter on the template. Use utility scissors to cut out the templates, cutting exactly on the drawn lines. When placing templates on the fabrics, pay careful attention to the grain line noted on each template. *Carefully* cut around each shape with a rotary cutter. You'll find it helpful to nest the template shapes across the fabric in order to make the best use of the fabric.

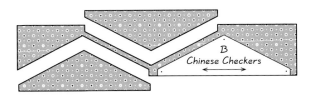

## PAPER-PIECING GUIDELINES

The quilt "Shadow Star" on page 42 uses paper-piecing methods to stitch the blocks together. The paper foundation stabilizes the patchwork, making it easier to sew the long, narrow points. While paper piecing can seem confusing at first, once you get the knack of the technique, it can be quite fun. The project instructions walk you through the specifics, but here are some tips to keep in mind to help you avoid any glitches.

- You'll need one paper-foundation pattern for each block. To ensure accuracy, be sure to make all copies for your quilt project on the same copy machine. Select paper that you can see through easily, holds up while sewing, and is easy to remove afterward. For example, a lightweight paper or paper made specifically for foundation piecing, such as Papers for Foundation Piecing available from Martingale & Company, are good choices. After photocopying the block, trim the paper foundation ¼" from the outer (cutting) line. (For a 6" finished block, the trimmed paper foundation would measure 7".)

- When cut as directed, all the fabric pieces will be large enough to cover the intended area on the paper foundation, including seam allowances.

- Prepare your sewing machine with a size 90/14 sewing-machine needle and an open-toe presser foot. Then adjust your stitch length to 14 to 16 stitches per inch. The larger needle and shorter stitch length will allow you to remove the paper easily. Don't make the stitches too short, however, because this will make removing stitches difficult if you sew a piece incorrectly.

- Set up a pressing area next to your sewing machine. Cover your pressing surface with a piece of scrap fabric to protect it from any toner that may transfer from the photocopies. Use a small travel iron set on a dry, cotton setting.

- If you need to repair a torn foundation paper, use removable tape. Be careful to not iron directly on the tape.

### TECHNIQUE TIP

To check the suitability of your foundation paper, thread your sewing machine and adjust the stitch length as instructed above. Sew through a single sheet of paper. If the paper tears as you sew, it is too flimsy to use for foundation piecing. If you try to tear the paper away from the stitched line and it doesn't tear away easily, the paper is too strong.

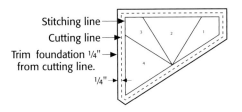

# Assembling the Quilt Top

After you have made all the blocks and cut the sashing or setting pieces as needed, you are ready to assemble the quilt top as directed in the specific project.

## QUILTS WITH BLOCKS SET SIDE BY SIDE

1. Arrange the blocks in rows as shown in the assembly diagram for your project.

2. Sew the blocks together in horizontal rows. Press the seams in opposite directions from one row to the next, unless instructed otherwise. If you are alternating plain blocks with pieced blocks, press all seams toward the plain blocks.

Quilt with blocks set side by side

3. Pin the rows together, carefully matching the seams from row to row. Sew the rows together and press the seams all in one direction, unless instructed otherwise.

## QUILTS WITH SASHING UNITS AND CORNER SQUARES

For quilts with sashing units and corner squares, measure the blocks, including seam allowances, and trim the sashing units as needed to match the block measurement. Follow the assembly diagram for your project to arrange the blocks, sashing strips, and corner squares as shown. Join the blocks and vertical sashing strips in rows, pressing the seams toward the sashing strips. Join the horizontal sashing strips and the corner squares in rows, once again pressing the seams toward the sashing strips. Sew the rows together and press the seams toward the sashing unit/corner square rows.

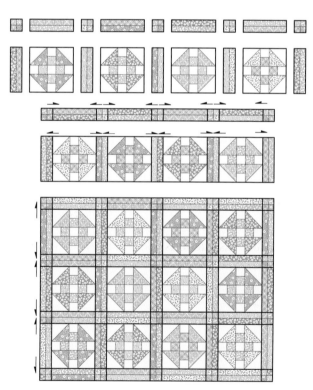

Quilt with sashing units and corner squares

# QUILTS SET DIAGONALLY

The blocks for diagonal settings are placed on point and arranged in diagonal rows. Corner and setting triangles are then added to fill in the side and corner spaces.

1 Arrange the blocks, sashing units (if applicable), setting triangles, and corner triangles as shown in the assembly diagram for your project.

2 Sew the blocks, sashing units (if applicable), and side setting triangles together in diagonal rows. Press as directed in the project instructions.

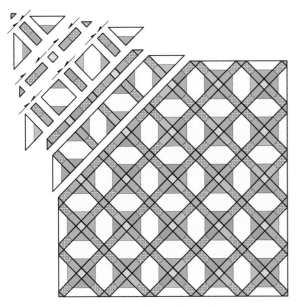

Quilt set diagonally

3 Sew the rows together, matching the seams from row to row. Press as directed in the project instructions. Sew the corner triangles on last and press the seams toward the corner triangles.

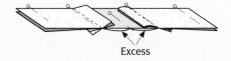

## TECHNIQUE TIP

When assembling the quilt top, you may discover that blocks and/or blocks and borders intended to match may vary slightly in size. To ease the pieces together, pin the ends, the points to match, and in between as needed to distribute the excess fabric. Sew with the shortest piece on top; the action of the feed dogs will ease the fullness of the bottom piece.

Excess

# BORDERS

Most quilts have a border or borders that frame the blocks. Borders can be simple strips of one or more fabrics. They can also be pieced or appliquéd and used in combination with plain strips.

Prepare border strips a few inches longer than you'll actually need; then trim them to the correct length once you know the dimensions of the center of your quilt top. To find the correct measurement for the border strips, always measure through the center of the quilt, not at the outside edges. This ensures that the borders are of equal length on opposite sides of the quilt and helps keep your quilt square.

Borders wider than 2" are usually cut on the lengthwise grain (parallel to the selvage) so they don't stretch and don't need to be pieced. You'll save fabric if you attach the borders to the longer sides of the quilt top first, and then attach them to the remaining two sides.

For quilts smaller than 40" square, or if you don't have enough fabric to cut the strips from the lengthwise grain, strips cut on the crosswise grain (across the fabric from selvage to selvage) work perfectly fine.

Borders less than 2" wide are usually cut from the crosswise grain and joined end to end with a diagonal seam to achieve the required length. This is the most fabric-efficient way to cut narrow border strips.

## Measuring for Length of Border Strips

❶ Measure the length of the quilt top from top to bottom through the center. Cut two border strips to this measurement, piecing as necessary.

Measure the center of the quilt, top to bottom.

❷ Mark the center of the border strips and the sides of the quilt top. Pin the borders to the sides of the quilt top, matching centers and ends. Ease or slightly stretch the quilt top to fit the border strips as necessary. Sew the side borders in place with a ¼"-wide seam and press the seams toward the border strips.

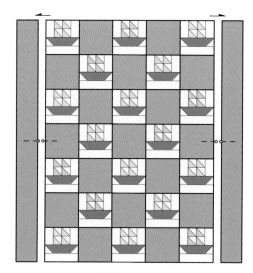

Mark centers.

❸ Measure the width of the quilt top from side to side through the center (including the side borders just added) to determine the length of the top and bottom border strips. Cut two border strips to this measurement, piecing as necessary. Mark the center of the border strips and the top and bottom of the quilt top. Pin the borders to the top and bottom of the quilt top, matching centers and ends. Ease or slightly stretch the quilt to fit the border strips as necessary. Sew the top and bottom borders in place with a ¼"-wide seam and press the seams toward the border strips.

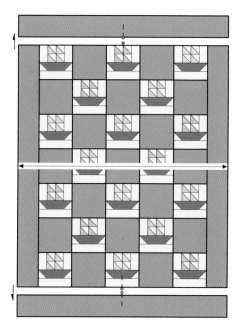

Measure the center of the quilt, side to side, including the borders. Mark centers.

# FINISHING YOUR QUILT

A quilt consists of three layers—the quilt top, backing, and batting. Once your quilt top is done, you are ready to move on to the finishing stages.

## BACKING AND BATTING

For the quilt backing, cut a piece of fabric 4" to 6" larger than the quilt top (2" to 3" on all sides). For quilts wider than the width of your fabric, you'll need to piece the backing. For most quilts in this book, I've listed enough backing fabric to piece the backing with one horizontal seam, leaving enough leftover fabric to cut a hanging sleeve. (Exceptions are noted when it makes better use of the fabric to run the seam vertically.) When piecing the backing, be sure to trim off the selvages before sewing the pieces together and press the seam open to reduce the bulk.

There are many types of batting to choose from. The type of batting you choose will depend on whether you plan to hand or machine quilt your quilt top. New battings are always being developed, so check with your favorite quilt shop for the most recent products. Generally, the thinner the batting—whether cotton or polyester—the easier it is to hand quilt. For machine quilting, a cotton batting works best. It won't move or slip between the quilt top and backing. Whatever type of batting you choose, the piece should be large enough to allow an extra 2" around all edges of the quilt top.

## TECHNIQUE TIP

To join two pieces of batting, place them on a flat surface, overlapping the two pieces 5" to 6". Use utility scissors to cut the overlapped edges in a wavy line. Remove the "waste" pieces and carefully re-position the batting pieces, nestling—but not overlapping—the curved edges together. Use a needle and thread to join the pieces with a large herringbone stitch or cross-stitch.

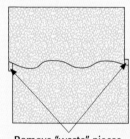 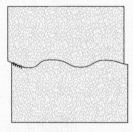

Remove "waste" pieces.

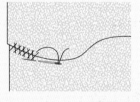

## LAYERING AND QUILTING THE QUILT

Before you layer the quilt, give the quilt top and backing a careful pressing. Then spread the backing, wrong side up, on a flat, clean surface. Anchor the backing with pins or masking tape, taking care not to stretch the fabric out of shape. Center the batting over the backing, smoothing out any wrinkles. Center the pressed quilt top, right side up, over the batting, smoothing out any wrinkles and making sure the edges of the quilt top are parallel to the edges of the backing. Note that you should always smooth from the center out and along straight lines to ensure that the blocks and borders remain straight.

For hand quilting, baste with needle and thread, starting in the center of the quilt and working diagonally to each corner. Continue basting in a grid of horizontal and vertical lines 6" to 8" apart. To finish, baste around the edges about ⅛" from the edge of the quilt top.

For machine quilting, baste the layers with size #2 rustproof safety pins. Place pins 4" to 6" apart; try to avoid areas where you intend to quilt. Finish by machine basting around the edges about ⅛" from the edge of the quilt top.

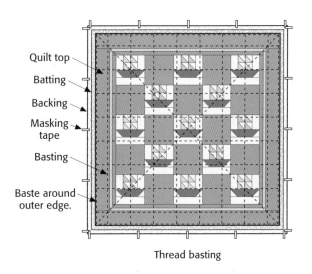

Thread basting

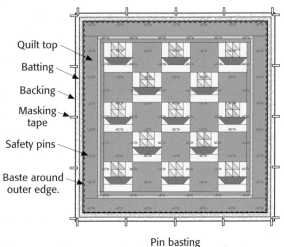

Pin basting

As a rule, no unquilted area should exceed 4" x 4". In addition, check the package of the batting that you're using for the recommendations

concerning the appropriate amount of quilting. The density of quilting should be similar throughout the entire quilt so that the quilt will remain square and will not become distorted.

To quilt by hand, you'll need short, sturdy needles (called Betweens), quilting thread, and a thimble to fit the middle finger of your sewing hand. Most quilters use a frame or hoop to support their work. Use the smallest needle you can comfortably handle; the finer the needle, the smaller your stitches will be. For excellent guidance regarding all aspects of hand-quilting techniques, see *Loving Stitches: A Guide to Fine Hand Quilting, Revised Edition* by Jeana Kimball (Martingale & Company, 2003).

Machine quilting is suitable for all types and sizes of quilts and allows you to complete a quilt quickly. For straight-line quilting, it is extremely helpful to have a walking foot to help feed the layers through the machine without shifting or puckering. For free-motion quilting, you need a darning foot and the ability to drop the feed dogs on your machine. With free-motion quilting, you don't turn the fabric under the needle but instead guide the fabric in the direction of the design. Because the feed dogs are lowered, the stitch length is determined by the speed at which you run the machine and feed the fabric under the foot. For more information on machine quilting, refer to *Machine Quilting Made Easy!* by Maurine Noble (Martingale & Company, 1994).

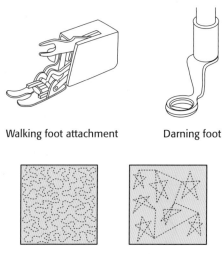

Walking foot attachment          Darning foot

Free-motion quilting designs

# SQUARING UP YOUR QUILT

When you complete the quilting, you'll need to trim the excess backing and batting as well as square up your quilt before sewing on the binding. Make sure all of the basting thread or pins have been removed from the center of the quilt, but leave the basting stitches around the outer edges. Align a ruler with the seam line of the outer border and measure the width of the outer border in several places. Using the narrowest measurement, position a ruler along the seam line of the outer border, and trim the excess batting and backing from all four sides. Use a large, square ruler to square up each corner.

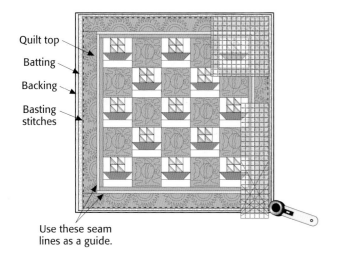

Quilt top
Batting
Backing
Basting stitches

Use these seam lines as a guide.

# MAKING A HANGING SLEEVE

If you plan to hang the finished quilt, attach a hanging sleeve or rod pocket to the back now, before you bind the quilt.

From the leftover backing fabric, cut an 8"-wide strip of fabric equal to the width of your quilt. On each short end of the strip, fold over ½", and then fold ½" again to make a hem. Press and stitch by machine.

Fold the strip in half lengthwise, wrong sides together; baste the raw edges to the top edge of the back of your quilt. These raw edges will be secured when you sew on the binding. Your quilt should be about 1" wider than the sleeve on both ends.

Make a little pleat in the sleeve to accommodate the thickness of the rod, and then slipstitch the ends and bottom edge of the sleeve to the backing fabric. This keeps the rod from being inserted next to the quilt backing.

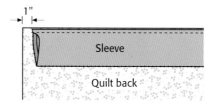

1"

Sleeve

Quilt back

# BINDING YOUR QUILT

The binding is a wonderful opportunity to add to the overall look of your quilt. If you want the binding to disappear, just use the same fabric for the binding as for the outer border. If you prefer the binding to frame the outer border or act as an additional border, then use a fabric different from the outer border.

Strips for binding are generally cut 2" to 2½" wide across the width of the fabric, depending on your preference for binding width and your choice of batting. (I used 2"-wide strips for the quilts in this book.) Cut enough strips to go around the perimeter of your quilt plus about 10" extra for making seams and turning corners.

❶ To make one long continuous strip, piece the strips at right angles and stitch across the top strip diagonally as shown. Trim the excess fabric, leaving a ¼"-wide seam allowance, and press the seams open.

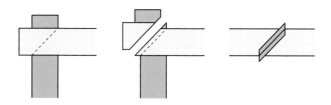

❷ Cut one end of the binding strip at a 45° angle. Press the binding strip in half lengthwise, wrong sides together and with raw edges aligned.

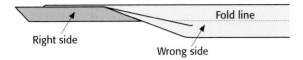

Fold line

Right side

Wrong side

## TECHNIQUE TIP

After piecing and pressing the long binding strip, accordion-fold the strip and secure it with a binder clip. This will prevent your binding strip from becoming tangled and frayed at the edges.

❸ Beginning with the angled end of the binding strip, align the raw edge of the strip with the raw edge of the quilt. Start on the bottom edge of the quilt (not in a corner) and pin. Using a walking foot and a ¼"-wide seam, begin stitching the binding to the quilt 8" from the strip's angled end. Stop ¼" from the first corner and backstitch.

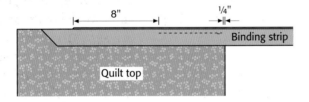

8"    ¼"

Binding strip

Quilt top

❹ Remove the quilt from the sewing machine. Fold the binding away from the quilt at a 45° angle, and then fold again and pin as shown to create an angled pleat at the corner. Begin with a backstitch at the fold of the binding and continue stitching along the edge of the quilt top, mitering each corner as you come to it.

❺ Stop stitching approximately 12" from the starting end of the binding strip; backstitch. Remove the quilt from the machine. Place the quilt on a flat surface and layer the beginning (angled) tail on top of the ending tail. Mark the ending tail where it meets the beginning tail. Make a second mark ½" to the right of the first mark.

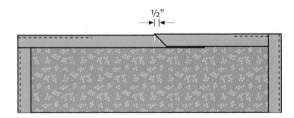

½"

**6** Open the ending tail strip and align the 45° line of a small Bias Square with the top edge of the opened binding strip. Place the corner of the ruler on the second mark. Cut the ending tail strip along the edge of the ruler as shown. The ends of both binding strips will form 45° angles and overlap ½".

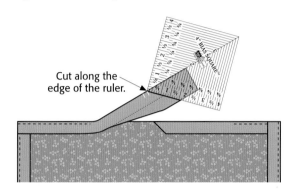

Cut along the edge of the ruler.

**7** Place the binding ends right sides together, aligning the angled raw edges as shown. Fold the quilt out of the way and stitch the ends together using a ¼" seam allowance. Press the seam open, refold the binding, and press the fold. Finish stitching the binding to the quilt top.

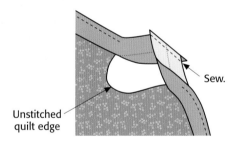

Sew.

Unstitched quilt edge

**8** Turn the binding to the back of the quilt. Using thread to match the binding, hand stitch the binding in place so that the folded edge covers the row of machine stitching. At each corner, fold the binding to form a miter on the back of the quilt.

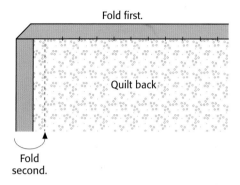

Fold first.

Quilt back

Fold second.

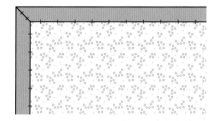

## ADDING A LABEL

A label provides important information, including the name of the quilt, the person who made it, and when and where the quilt was made. You may also want to include the name of the recipient, if the quilt is a gift, and any other interesting or important information. A label can be as elaborate or as simple as you desire. You can sign your name on the back of the finished quilt using a permanent marker, purchase pretty labels that are printed on fabric, or make your own label. You'll find lots of ideas and instruction for labels in *One-of-a-Kind Quilt Labels: Unique Ideas for a Special Finishing Touch* by Thea Nerud (Martingale & Company, 2004).

# SPRING NEST

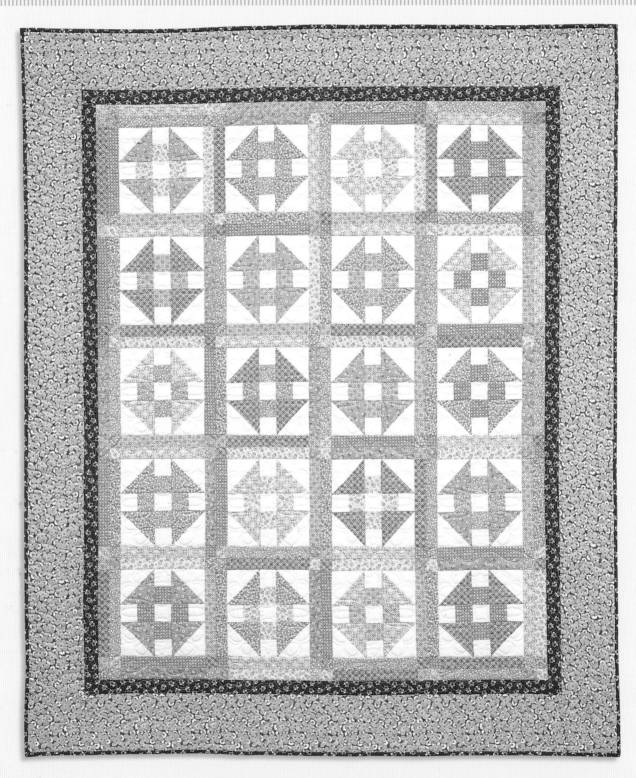

By Nancy Mahoney. Quilted by Dawn Kelly.

Finished Quilt Size: 52½" x 62"  •  Finished Block Size: 7½"

Eveline Foland, a designer for the *Kansas City Star*, created the Crow's Nest pattern in 1932. The newspaper described the pattern as a "pretty block which has quite an air of being much more elaborate than it is really." The soft lavender and yellow colors of this playful quilt herald the arrival of spring. The results combine the homey familiarity of a traditional pattern with updated methods that make the piecing as easy as can be!

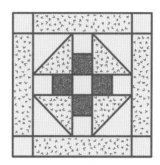

Crow's Nest

## Materials

*Yardages are based on 42"-wide fabrics.*

1¾ yards of lavender floral print for outer border

⅜ yard *each* of 4 assorted lavender prints for blocks and sashing

⅜ yard *each* of 4 assorted yellow prints for blocks and sashing

⅞ yard of cream solid for blocks and sashing

¾ yard of dark lavender print for inner border and binding

3½ yards of fabric for backing

56" x 66" piece of batting

## Cutting

*All measurements include ¼"-wide seam allowances. Cut all strips across the width of the fabric (selvage to selvage) unless instructed otherwise.*

**From the cream solid, cut:**
4 strips, 2" x 42"

4 strips, 3⅞" x 42"; crosscut into 40 squares, 3⅞" x 3⅞"

1 strip, 2" x 42"; crosscut into 20 squares, 2" x 2"

**From *each* of the 4 assorted yellow prints, cut:**
1 strip, 2" x 42" (4 total)

3 strips, 1½" x 42" (12 total)

1 strip, 1½" x 24" (4 total)

**From *each* of the 4 assorted lavender prints, cut:**
1 strip, 3⅞" x 42"; crosscut into 10 squares, 3⅞" x 3⅞" (40 total)

3 strips, 1½" x 42" (12 total)

1 strip, 1½" x 24" (4 total)

**From the dark lavender print, cut:**
5 strips, 1¾" x 42"

6 strips, 2" x 42"

**From the *lengthwise grain* of the lavender floral print, cut:**
4 strips, 5½" x 58"

## Making the Blocks

For detailed instructions, refer to "Making Units from Strip Sets" on page 8 and "Half-Square-Triangle Units" on page 9.

1. Sew a 2" x 42" cream strip and a 2" x 42" assorted yellow strip together to a make a strip set; press. Make four strip sets. Cut the strip sets into 2"-wide segments. Cut 80 segments in matching sets of four.

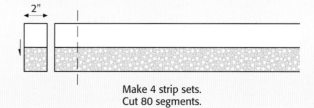

2"

Make 4 strip sets.
Cut 80 segments.

2. Draw a diagonal line from corner to corner on the wrong side of each 3⅞" cream square. Place a marked cream square on a 3⅞" lavender square, right sides together, and stitch ¼" on each side of the marked diagonal line. Cut on the line to make two half-square-triangle units; press. Make 80 half-square-triangle units. Each unit should measure 3½" x 3½".

Make 80.

3. Arrange four matching segments from step 1, four matching units from step 2, and one 2" cream square as shown. Sew the segments, units, and square together in rows; press. Sew the rows together; press. Make 20 blocks.

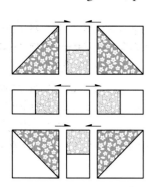 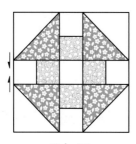

Make 20.

## Making the Sashing and Corner Squares

1. Sew a 1½" x 42" assorted yellow strip and a 1½" x 42" assorted lavender strip together to make a strip set; press. Make 10 scrappy strip sets. Cut the strip sets into 8"-wide segments. Cut 49 segments. You'll have four strips left over—two in yellow and two in lavender. Set them aside for another project.

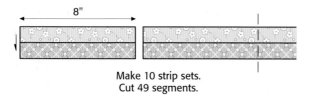

8"

Make 10 strip sets.
Cut 49 segments.

2. Sew one 1½" x 24" assorted yellow strip and one 1½" x 24" assorted lavender strip together to a make a strip set; press. Make four scrappy strip sets. Cut the strip sets into 1½"-wide segments. Cut 60 segments.

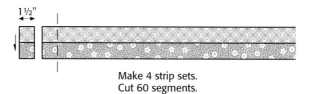

1½"

Make 4 strip sets.
Cut 60 segments.

3. Arrange two segments from step 2 as shown. Sew the segments together. Refer to the technique tip on page 10 for guidance on pressing the center seams. Make 30 scrappy four-patch units.

Make 30.

## Assembling the Quilt

For detailed instructions, refer to "Quilts with Sashing Units and Corner Squares" on page 12.

1. Arrange and sew together five sashing units and four blocks, alternating them as shown to make a block row; press. Referring to the assembly diagram on page 23 for placement of colors in the sashing units for each row, make five rows.

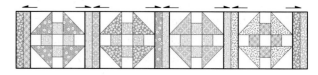

Make 5.

2. Arrange and sew together five four-patch units and four sashing units, alternating them as shown to make a sashing row; press. Referring to the assembly diagram for placement of colors in the sashing units and four-patch units for each row, make six rows.

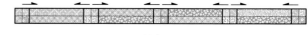

Make 6.

③ Sew the block rows and sashing rows together, alternating them as shown in the assembly diagram below. Press the seams toward the sashing rows.

Assembly diagram

## Adding the Borders

For detailed instructions, refer to "Borders" on pages 13–14.

① Join the 1¾"-wide dark lavender inner-border strips end to end to make a continuous strip. Measure the quilt through the center from top to bottom and cut two 1¾"-wide inner-border strips from the long strip to fit that measurement.

② Sew the cut inner-border strips to the side edges of the quilt top. Press toward the border strips.

③ Measure the quilt through the center from side to side, including the borders just added. Cut two 1¾"-wide dark lavender inner-border strips from the remainder of the long strip to fit that measurement.

④ Sew the cut inner-border strips to the top and bottom edges of the quilt top; press.

⑤ Measure the quilt through the center from top to bottom and trim two 5½"-wide lavender floral outer-border strips to fit that measurement.

⑥ Sew the trimmed outer-border strips to the side edges of the quilt top. Press toward the outer-border strips.

⑦ Measure the quilt through the center from side to side and trim the remaining 5½"-wide lavender floral outer-border strips to fit that measurement.

⑧ Sew the trimmed outer-border strips to the top and bottom edges of the quilt top; press.

## Finishing the Quilt

For detailed instructions on the following finishing techniques, refer to "Finishing Your Quilt" on page 15.

① Cut and piece the backing fabric so that it is 4" to 6" larger than the quilt top. Layer the quilt top with batting and backing. Baste the layers together.

② Hand or machine quilt as desired. You may wish to quilt a medallion pattern in each block, and a swirling design in the sashing. Finish by quilting a continuous feather design in the border.

③ Square up the quilt sandwich.

④ Add a hanging sleeve, if desired.

⑤ Use the 2"-wide dark lavender strips to make binding. Sew the binding to the quilt. Add a label, if desired.

# SUMMER SAILS

By Nancy Mahoney. Quilted by Dawn Kelly.

Finished Quilt Size: 51½" x 67½"  •  Finished Block Size: 8"

A reader of the *Kansas City Star* contributed this version of the sailboat motif. As described in the newspaper in 1936, "the Mayflower quilt block may be developed into a jolly design for a boy's room." This updated version takes the traditional technique a step further, using only squares and rectangles to create the cheery blocks.

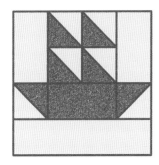

Mayflower

# Materials

*Yardages are based on 42"-wide fabrics. Fat quarters measure 18" x 21".*

2⅞ yards of blue-and-yellow print for setting squares and inner and outer borders

1⅜ yards of cream solid for blocks

1 fat quarter *each* of 3 assorted blue prints for blocks

1 fat quarter *each* of 3 assorted yellow prints for blocks

⅜ yard of dark yellow print for middle border

½ yard of dark blue print for binding

3½ yards of fabric for backing

55" x 72" piece of batting

# Cutting

*All measurements include ¼"-wide seam allowances. Cut all strips across the width of the fabric (selvage to selvage) unless instructed otherwise.*

**From the cream solid, cut:**
3 strips, 2⅞" x 42"; crosscut into 36 squares, 2⅞" x 2⅞"

5 strips, 2½" x 42"; crosscut into 36 rectangles, 2½" x 4½"

3 strips, 2½" x 42"; crosscut into 36 squares, 2½" x 2½"

5 strips, 2½" x 42"; crosscut into 18 rectangles, 2½" x 8½"

**From *each* of the 3 assorted yellow prints, cut:**
2 strips, 2⅞" x 21"; crosscut into 12 squares, 2⅞" x 2⅞" (36 total)

**From *each* of the 3 assorted blue prints, cut:**
3 strips, 2½" x 21"; crosscut into 6 rectangles, 2½" x 8½" (18 total)

**From the *lengthwise grain* of the blue-and-yellow print, cut:**
4 strips, 1½" x 60"

4 strips, 4½" x 64"

**From the remaining blue-and-yellow print, cut:**
17 squares, 8½" x 8½"

**From the dark yellow print, cut:**
6 strips, 1¼" x 42"

**From the dark blue print, cut:**
7 strips, 2" x 42"

# Making the Blocks

For detailed instructions, refer to "Half-Square-Triangle Units" and "Cut Corners" on pages 9–10.

① Draw a diagonal line from corner to corner on the wrong side of each 2⅞" cream square. Place a marked cream square on a 2⅞" yellow square, right sides together, and stitch ¼" on each side of the marked diagonal line. Cut on the line to make two half-square-triangle units; press. Make 72 half-square-triangle units. Each unit should measure 2½" x 2½".

Make 72.

② Sew four matching units from step 1 together as shown. Refer to the technique tip on page 10 for guidance on pressing the center seams. Make 18.

Make 18.

③ Sew one unit from step 2 between two 2½" x 4½" cream rectangles as shown; press. Make 18.

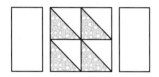

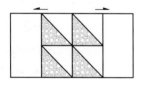

Make 18.

④ Draw a diagonal line from corner to corner on the wrong side of each 2½" cream square. Align a marked square with each end of a 2½" x 8½" blue rectangle, right sides together. Stitch on the marked diagonal line. Trim ¼" from the stitching line; press. Make 18.

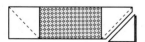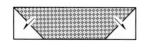

Make 18.

⑤ Sew one unit from step 4 and a 2½" x 8½" cream rectangle together as shown; press. Make 18.

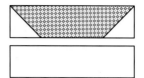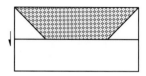

Make 18.

⑥ Sew one unit from step 3 and one unit from step 5 together as shown; press. Make 18 blocks.

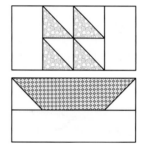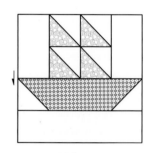

Make 18.

## Assembling the Quilt

For detailed instructions, refer to "Quilts with Blocks Set Side by Side" on page 12.

① Arrange the blocks and 8½" blue-and-yellow squares into seven horizontal rows of five blocks each, alternating the blocks and squares in each row and from row to row as shown in the assembly diagram on the facing page.

② Sew the blocks and squares into rows as shown in the assembly diagram. Press the seams toward the blue-and-yellow squares. Stitch the rows together. Press the seams in one direction.

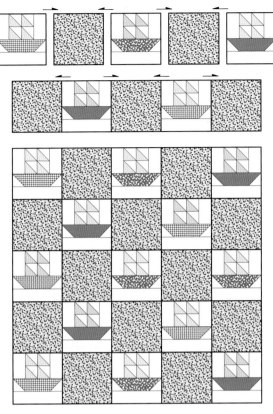

Assembly diagram

## Adding the Borders

For detailed instructions, refer to "Borders" on pages 13–14.

1. Measure the quilt through the center from top to bottom and trim two 1½"-wide blue-and-yellow inner-border strips to fit that measurement.

2. Sew the trimmed inner-border strips to the side edges of the quilt top. Press toward the border strips.

3. Measure the quilt through the center from side to side, including the borders just added. Trim the remaining 1½"-wide blue-and-yellow inner-border strips to fit that measurement.

4. Sew the trimmed inner-border strips to the top and bottom edges of the quilt top; press.

5. Join the 1¼"-wide dark yellow middle-border strips end to end to make a continuous strip. Measure the quilt through the center from top to bottom and cut two 1¼"-wide middle-border strips from the long strip to fit that measurement.

6. Sew the cut middle-border strips to the side edges of the quilt top. Press toward the middle-border strips.

7. Measure the quilt through the center from side to side. Cut two 1¼"-wide dark yellow middle-border strips from the remainder of the long strip to fit that measurement.

8. Sew the cut middle-border strips to the top and bottom edges of the quilt top; press.

9. Repeat steps 1–4 to measure, trim, and sew the 4½"-wide blue-and-yellow outer-border strips to the sides, top, and bottom of the quilt. Press toward the outer-border strips.

## Finishing the Quilt

For detailed instructions on the following finishing techniques, refer to "Finishing Your Quilt" on page 15.

1. Cut and piece the backing fabric so that it is 4" to 6" larger than the quilt top. Layer the quilt top with batting and backing. Baste the layers together.

2. Hand or machine quilt as desired. You may wish to quilt swirls and waves in each block, and a swirling design with fun fish motifs in the large squares. Finish by quilting a sunburst motif in the border.

3. Square up the quilt sandwich.

4. Add a hanging sleeve, if desired.

5. Use the 2"-wide dark blue strips to make binding. Sew the binding to the quilt. Add a label, if desired.

# GARDEN STEPS

By Nancy Mahoney. Quilted by Dawn Kelly.

Finished Quilt Size: 65½" x 83½"  •  Finished Block Size: 9"

The block in this quilt has many names: Jacob's Ladder, Stepping Stones, Underground Railroad, Wagon Tracks, and several more. As printed in the *Kansas City Star* in 1934, this pattern was a gift from a quilt fan and was described as "a new expression of a very old theme, Jacob's Ladder, attractive in any two colors." Call it what you will, it's charming in any colors you choose. Notice how using different colors for the "steps" adds visual interest to the quilt. Shortcut techniques make stitching this one a breeze!

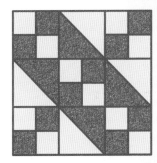

Jacob's Ladder

## Materials

*Yardages are based on 42"-wide fabrics. Fat quarters measure 18" x 21" and fat eighths measure 9" x 21".*

2½ yards of cream solid for blocks

2⅜ yards of blue floral print for outer border

1 fat quarter *each* of 8 assorted green prints for blocks

1 fat eighth *each* of 16 assorted pink prints for blocks

1 fat eighth *each* of 16 assorted blue prints for blocks

⅞ yard of pink solid for inner border and binding

5 yards of fabric for backing

70" x 88" piece of batting

## Cutting

*All measurements include ¼"-wide seam allowances. Cut all strips across the width of the fabric (selvage to selvage) unless instructed otherwise.*

**From the cream solid, cut:**
10 strips, 3⅞" x 42"; crosscut into 96 squares, 3⅞" x 3⅞"

40 strips, 2" x 20"

**From *each* of the 8 assorted green prints, cut:**
3 strips, 3⅞" x 20"; crosscut into 12 squares, 3⅞" x 3⅞" (96 total)

**From *each* of the 16 assorted pink prints, cut:**
2 strips, 2" x 20" (32 total)

**From *each* of the 16 assorted blue prints, cut:**
2 strips, 2" x 20" (32 total)

**From the pink solid, cut:**
7 strips, 1¼" x 42"

8 strips, 2" x 42"

**From the *lengthwise grain* of the blue floral print, cut:**
4 strips, 5½" x 80"

## Making the Blocks

For detailed instructions, refer to "Half-Square-Triangle Units" on page 9 and "Making Units from Strip Sets" on page 8.

1 Draw a diagonal line from corner to corner on the wrong side of each 3⅞" cream square. Place a marked cream square on a green 3⅞" square, right sides together, and stitch ¼" on each side of the marked diagonal line. Cut on

the line to make two half-square-triangle units; press. Make 192 half-square-triangle units. Each unit should measure 3½" x 3½".

Make 192.

❷ Sew a 2" x 20" cream strip and a 2" x 20" assorted pink strip together to a make a strip set; press. Make 20 strip sets. Cut the strip sets into 2"-wide segments. Cut 192 segments.

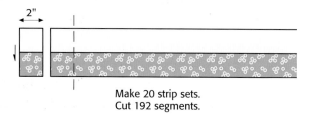

2"

Make 20 strip sets.
Cut 192 segments.

❸ Sew a 2" x 20" cream strip and a 2" x 20" assorted blue strip together to a make a strip set; press. Make 20 strip sets. Cut the strip sets into 2" segments. Cut 192 segments.

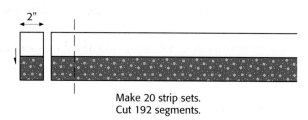

2"

Make 20 strip sets.
Cut 192 segments.

❹ Sew a 2" x 20" assorted blue strip and a 2" x 20" assorted pink strip together to a make a strip set; press. Make 10 strip sets. Cut the strip sets into 2"-wide segments. Cut 96 segments. You'll have four strips left over—two in pink and two in blue. Set them aside for another project.

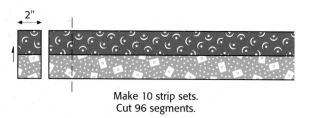

2"

Make 10 strip sets.
Cut 96 segments.

❺ Sew two segments from steps 2, 3, or 4 together as shown to make the required number of scrappy four-patch units in each variation. Refer to the technique tip on page 10 for guidance on pressing the center seams.

Make 96.　　　Make 96.　　　Make 48.

❻ Arrange four units from step 1, two pink/cream four-patch units, two blue/cream four-patch units, and one blue/pink four-patch unit from step 5 as shown. Sew the units together in rows; press. Sew the rows together; press. Make 48.

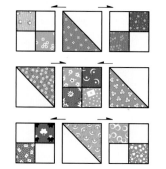 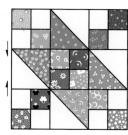

Make 48.

## Assembling the Quilt

For detailed instructions, refer to "Quilts with Blocks Set Side by Side" on page 12.

❶ Arrange the blocks in eight horizontal rows of six blocks each. Rotate every other block 90° so that the four-patch units form diagonal lines across the quilt as shown in the assembly diagram on the facing page.

❷ Sew the blocks into rows. Press the seams in alternate directions from row to row. Stitch the rows together. Press the seams in one direction.

Assembly diagram

## Adding the Borders

For detailed instructions, refer to "Borders" on pages 13–14.

❶ Join the 1¼"-wide pink solid inner-border strips end to end to make a continuous strip. Measure the quilt through the center from top to bottom and cut two 1¼"-wide inner-border strips from the long strip to fit that measurement.

❷ Sew the cut inner-border strips to the side edges of the quilt top. Press toward the border strips.

❸ Measure the quilt through the center from side to side, including the borders just added. Cut two 1¼"-wide pink solid inner-border strips from the remainder of the long strip to fit that measurement.

❹ Sew the cut inner-border strips to the top and bottom edges of the quilt top; press.

❺ Measure the quilt through the center from top to bottom and trim two 5½"-wide blue floral outer-border strips to fit that measurement.

❻ Sew the trimmed outer-border strips to the side edges of the quilt top. Press toward the outer-border strips.

❼ Measure the quilt through the center from side to side and trim the remaining 5½"-wide blue floral outer-border strips to fit that measurement.

❽ Sew the trimmed outer-border strips to the top and bottom edges of the quilt top; press.

## Finishing the Quilt

For detailed instructions on the following finishing techniques, refer to "Finishing Your Quilt" on page 15.

❶ Cut and piece the backing fabric so that it is 4" to 6" larger than the quilt top. Layer the quilt top with batting and backing (vertical seam). Baste the layers together.

❷ Hand or machine quilt as desired. You may wish to quilt an allover design of ovals, loops, flowers, leaves, and swags on the body of the quilt. Finish by quilting a continuous leaf design in the border.

❸ Square up the quilt sandwich.

❹ Add a hanging sleeve, if desired.

❺ Use the 2"-wide pink strips to make the binding. Sew the binding to the quilt. Add a label, if desired.

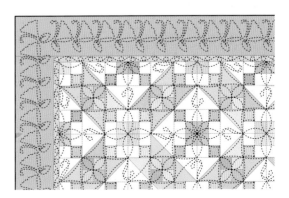

# HOLLYHOCKS IN BLOOM

By Nancy Mahoney

Finished Quilt Size: 60¾" x 60¾"  •  Finished Block Size: 5"

The pattern for this design was printed in the *Kansas City Star* in 1936. The newspaper described it as "an interesting design for an allover pattern. The 'Chinese Puzzle' makes a lovely quilt and may be developed in a variety of color schemes." However, like many patterns of the time, the pieces were not a common size and were difficult to piece together. This version is easy to piece using updated techniques and rotary-cutting instructions. Use a variety of pink prints to add interest to your blooming flowers.

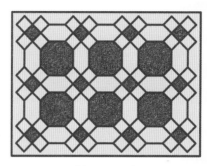

Chinese Puzzle

# Materials

*Yardages are based on 42"-wide fabrics. Fat quarters measure 18" x 21" and fat eighths measure 9" x 21".*

3 yards of green trellis print for sashing, inner border, outer border, and binding*

1⅝ yards of cream background print for blocks

1 fat quarter *each* of 5 assorted pink prints for blocks

1 fat eighth *each* of 4 assorted pink prints for blocks

1 fat quarter of green floral print for sashing squares and sashing triangles

1 fat eighth of yellow solid for sashing squares

⅜ yard of pink floral print for middle border

3⅝ yards of fabric for backing

65" x 65" piece of batting

*\*If your fabric measures a true 42" after it has been washed and the selvages have been trimmed, you will only need 2⅜ yards of this fabric.*

# Cutting

*All measurements include ¼"-wide seam allowances. Cut all strips across the width of the fabric (selvage to selvage) unless instructed otherwise.*

**From *each* of the 5 fat quarters of assorted pink prints, cut:**
2 strips, 3" x 21"; crosscut into 12 squares, 3" x 3" (60 total)

2 strips, 3" x 21" (10 total)

**From *each* of the 4 fat eighths of assorted pink prints, cut:**
2 strips, 3" x 21"; crosscut into 10 squares, 3" x 3" (40 total)

**From the cream background print, cut:**
6 strips, 5½" x 42"; crosscut into 40 squares, 5½" x 5½"

5 squares, 8⅜" x 8 ⅜"; crosscut twice diagonally to yield 20 quarter-square triangles

**From the *lengthwise grain* of the green trellis print, cut:**
4 inner-border strips, 2" x 55"

4 strips, 5½" x 65"

4 binding strips, 2" x 65"

**From the remaining green trellis print, cut:**
10 strips, 3" x 21"

From the yellow solid, cut:

3 strips, 2" x 21"; crosscut into 25 squares, 2" x 2"

From the green floral print, cut:

2 strips, 2" x 21"; crosscut into 16 squares, 2" x 2"

4 squares, 3⅜" x 3⅜"; cut twice diagonally to yield 16 quarter-square triangles

2 squares, 2" x 2"; cut once diagonally to yield 4 half-square triangles

From the pink floral print, cut:

6 strips, 1¼" x 42"

## Making the Blocks and Half Blocks

For detailed instructions, refer to "Cut Corners" on pages 9–10.

1. Draw a diagonal line from corner to corner on the wrong side of each 3" assorted pink square. Align a marked square with opposite corners of each 5½" cream square, right sides together. Stitch on the marked diagonal line. Trim ¼" from the stitching line; press. Make 40 blocks. You'll have 20 pink squares left over and will use them in the next step.

Make 40.

2. Align a remaining marked pink square from step 1 with the right-angle corner of each 8⅜" cream triangle, right sides together. Stitch on the marked diagonal line. Trim ¼" from the stitching line; press. Make 20 half blocks.

Make 20.

## Making the Sashing Units

For detailed instructions, refer to "Making Units from Strip Sets" on page 8. Sew a 3" x 21" assorted pink strip and a 3" x 21" green trellis strip together to make a strip set; press. Make 10 strip sets. Cut the strip sets into 2"-wide segments. Cut 100 segments, which will be called sashing units.

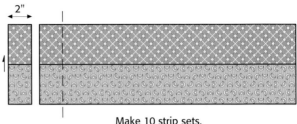

Make 10 strip sets.
Cut 100 segments.

## Assembling the Quilt

For detailed instructions, refer to "Quilts Set Diagonally" on page 13.

1. Arrange the blocks, half blocks, sashing units, 2" yellow sashing squares, and 2" green floral sashing squares in diagonal rows as shown in the assembly diagram on the facing page. Add the 3⅜" green floral side sashing triangles and 2" green floral corner sashing triangles.

2. Sew the blocks, half blocks, and sashing units together in rows. Press toward the sashing units.

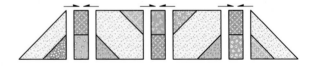

3. Sew the sashing units, sashing squares, and side sashing triangles together in rows. Press toward the sashing units.

4. Sew the block rows and sashing rows together. Press the seams toward the sashing rows. Add the corner sashing triangles last; press.

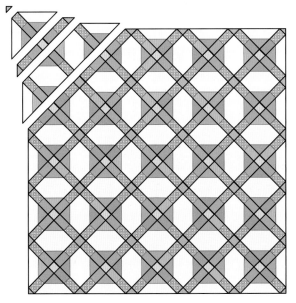

Assembly diagram

## Adding the Borders

For detailed instructions, refer to "Borders" on pages 13–14.

1. Measure the quilt through the center from top to bottom and trim two 2"-wide green trellis inner-border strips to fit that measurement.

2. Sew the trimmed inner-border strips to the side edges of the quilt top. Press toward the border strips.

3. Measure the quilt through the center from side to side, including the borders just added. Trim the remaining 2"-wide green trellis inner-border strips to fit that measurement.

4. Sew the trimmed inner-border strips to the top and bottom edges of the quilt top; press.

5. Join the 1¼"-wide pink floral middle-border strips end to end to make a continuous strip. Measure the quilt through the center from top to bottom and cut two 1¼"-wide middle-border strips from the long strip to fit that measurement.

6. Sew the cut middle-border strips to the side edges of the quilt. Press toward the middle-border strips.

7. Measure the quilt through the center from side to side. Cut two 1¼"-wide pink floral middle-border strips from the remainder of the long strip to fit that measurement.

8. Sew the cut middle-border strips to the top and bottom edges of the quilt; press.

9. Repeat steps 1–4 to measure, trim, and sew the 5½"-wide green trellis outer-border strips to the sides, top, and bottom of the quilt. Press toward the outer-border strips.

## Finishing the Quilt

For detailed instructions on the following finishing techniques, refer to "Finishing Your Quilt" on page 15.

1. Cut and piece the backing fabric so that it is 4" to 6" larger than the quilt top. Layer the quilt top with batting and backing. Baste the layers together.

2. Hand or machine quilt as desired. You may wish to quilt a medallion design in the center of each block and a medallion design over the pink triangles. Quilt the sashing and borders in the ditch, and add straight lines to the inner border. Finish by quilting a continuous leaf design in the outer border.

3. Square up the quilt sandwich.

4. Add a hanging sleeve, if desired.

5. Use the 2"-wide green trellis strips to make the binding. Sew the binding to the quilt. Add a label, if desired.

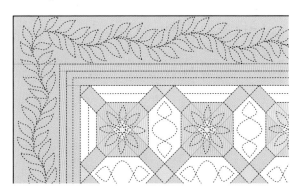

By Nancy Mahoney

Finished Quilt Size: 49" x 58"  •  Finished Block Size: 9"

The Treasure Chest block pattern was available from the *Houston Post* Household Arts Department for 10¢ in 1933. The newspaper's enticing description says it all: "This quilt is exciting for the quiltmaker, for it is made entirely of scraps put together in a hit-or-miss way. And what could be more fun—plenty of variety—an excellent way of treasuring scraps of all the dresses you were particularly fond of? It is most effective to follow the distribution of light and dark materials as illustrated, for this arrangement brings out the design best. Aside from all these pleasant features, Treasure Chest is easy to make, which is always of importance to the needlewoman." Of course, it's even easier to make in this updated version.

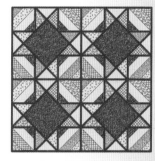

Treasure Chest (4 blocks)

## Materials

*Yardages are based on 42"-wide fabrics. Fat quarters measure 18" x 21" and fat eighths measure 9" x 21".*

1 fat quarter *each* of 5 assorted cream floral prints for blocks

1 fat quarter *each* of 5 assorted pink prints for blocks and outer border

1 fat quarter *each* of 5 assorted green prints for blocks and outer border

1 fat quarter *each* of 5 assorted lavender prints for blocks and outer border

1 fat quarter *each* of 5 assorted blue prints for blocks and binding

1 fat quarter *each* of 4 assorted medium cream prints for blocks

1 fat eighth *each* of 5 assorted light cream prints for blocks

⅜ yard of blue floral for inner border

3¼ yards of fabric for backing

53" x 63" piece of batting

## Cutting

*All measurements include ¼"-wide seam allowances. Cut all strips across the width of the fabric (selvage to selvage).*

**From *each* of the 5 assorted cream floral prints, cut:**
8 squares, 3⅞" x 3⅞" (40 total)

**From *each* of the 4 assorted medium cream prints, cut:**
10 squares, 3⅞" x 3⅞" (40 total)

**From the 5 assorted blue prints, cut a *total* of:**
48 squares, 2" x 2", in matching sets of 4
10 squares, 4¼" x 4¼"; cut 5 squares twice diagonally to yield 20 quarter-square triangles
5 squares, 4¾" x 4¾"
12 strips, 2" x 21"

**From the 5 assorted pink prints, cut a *total* of:**
40 squares, 2" x 2", in matching sets of 4
10 squares, 4¼" x 4¼"; cut 5 squares twice diagonally to yield 20 quarter-square triangles
5 squares, 4¾" x 4¾"
4 rectangles, 5½" x 18"

**From the 5 assorted green prints, cut a *total* of:**

48 squares, 2" x 2", in matching sets of 4

10 squares, 4¼" x 4¼"; cut 5 squares twice diagonally to yield 20 quarter-square triangles

5 squares, 4¾" x 4¾"

4 rectangles, 5½" x 18"

**From the 5 assorted lavender prints, cut a *total* of:**

24 squares, 2" x 2" in matching sets of 4

10 squares, 4¼" x 4¼"; cut 5 squares twice diagonally to yield 20 quarter-square triangles

5 squares, 4¾" x 4¾"

4 rectangles, 5½" x 18"

**From *each* of the 5 assorted light cream prints, cut:**

4 squares, 4¼" x 4¼" (20 total)

**From the blue floral, cut:**

5 strips, 2" x 42"

## Making the Blocks

For detailed instructions, refer to "Half-Square-Triangle Units" and "Cut Corners" on pages 9–10.

**1** Draw a diagonal line from corner to corner on the wrong side of each 3⅞" cream floral square. Place a marked cream square on a 3⅞" medium cream square, right sides together, and stitch ¼" on each side of the marked diagonal line. Cut on the line to make two half-square-triangle units; press. Make 80 half-square-triangle units in matching sets of 4. Each unit should measure 3½" x 3½".

Make 80.

**2** Draw a diagonal line from corner to corner on the wrong side of each 2" assorted blue, pink, green, and lavender square. Align a marked square on opposite corners of each unit from step 1, right sides together, as shown. Stitch on the marked diagonal line. Trim ¼" from the stitching line; press. Make 80 in matching sets of 4.

Make 80.

**3** Repeat step 1, drawing a diagonal line on the wrong side of each 4¼" light cream square and matching it with a 4¼" assorted blue, pink, green, or lavender square. Make 40 half-square-triangle units, each 3½" x 3½" in matching sets of 2. Cut each half-square-triangle unit once diagonally to make 80 quarter-square-triangle units as shown. (They will be mirror-images of each other and you will have 40 of each.)

Make 40.                Make 80
                (40 mirror-image pairs).

**4** Sew two matching mirror-image units from step 3 and one unit from step 2 together to make a side unit; press. Make 40 in matching pairs.

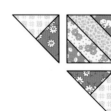 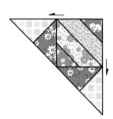

Make 40.

**⑤** Using the same combination of fabrics that you used in step 4, sew two 4¼" assorted blue, pink, green, or lavender triangles and one unit from step 2 together to make a corner unit; press. Make 40 in matching pairs.

Make 40.

**⑥** Arrange and sew two matching side units from step 4, two corner units from step 5 to match, and one 4¾" assorted blue, pink, green, or lavender square together as shown; press. Make 20 blocks.

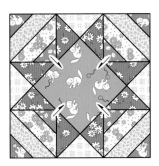

Make 20.

## Assembling the Quilt

For detailed instructions, refer to "Quilts with Blocks Set Side by Side" on page 12.

**❶** Arrange the blocks into five horizontal rows of four blocks each as shown in the assembly diagram below.

**❷** Sew the blocks into rows. Press the seams in alternate directions from row to row. Stitch the rows together. Press the seams in one direction.

Assembly diagram

## *Adding the Borders*

For detailed instructions, refer to "Borders" on pages 13–14.

**1** Join the 2"-wide blue floral inner-border strips end to end to make a continuous strip. Measure the quilt through the center from top to bottom and cut two border strips from the long strip to fit that measurement.

**2** Sew the cut inner-border strips to the side edges of the quilt top. Press toward the border strips.

**3** Measure the quilt through the center from side to side, including the borders just added. Cut two 2"-wide blue floral inner-border strips from the remainder of the long strip to fit that measurement.

**4** Sew the cut inner-border strips to the top and bottom edges of the quilt top; press.

**5** Refer to the photo on page 36 and the diagram below. Sew three 5½" x 18" pink rectangles end to end to make a border strip. Press the seams open. Repeat to sew two 5½" x 18" green rectangles and one 5½" x 18" lavender rectangle together; press.

**6** Measure the quilt through the center from top to bottom, including the inner borders just added. Trim the pieced border strips to that measurement and sew the pink border to the left edge of the quilt top and the green/lavender border to the right edge as shown. Press toward the pieced border strips.

**7** Repeat step 5, sewing one pink and two green rectangles together to make the top border strip and three lavender rectangles together to make the bottom border strip; press. Measure the quilt through the center from side to side, trim the pieced border strips, and sew them to the top and bottom edges of the quilt top; press.

## Finishing the Quilt

For detailed instructions on the following finishing techniques, refer to "Finishing Your Quilt" on page 15.

1. Cut and piece the backing fabric so that it is 4" to 6" larger than the quilt top. Layer the quilt top with batting and backing. Baste the layers together.

2. Hand or machine quilt as desired. You may wish to quilt the borders and blocks in the ditch and add a medallion design in the center square of each block. Finish by quilting an interlocking heart design in the border.

3. Square up the quilt sandwich.

4. Add a hanging sleeve, if desired.

5. Use the 2"-wide assorted blue strips to make the binding. Sew the binding to the quilt. Add a label, if desired.

# SHADOW STAR

By Nancy Mahoney

Finished Quilt Size: 53" x 59"  •  Finished Block Size: 6"

*Godey's Lady's Book* was a popular fashion magazine of the nineteenth century. It was one of the first magazines issued for women, and quilt designs appeared along with patterns for clothing and other household items. In 1859, one of these designs included the Light and Shadow block. The block was later reprinted in several newspapers from 1933 through 1937, and it has since been used by thousands of quiltmakers. The pattern was traditionally shown in a light and dark design similar to the one illustrated in "Design Options" on page 50. However, I knew I'd be bored using just two fabrics throughout, so I chose to make a scrappy design and use lots of fabrics. If you want to use fewer fabrics, cut more pieces from each print, or try one of the options shown on pages 47–50. I've also pieced the block using the foundation-paper method, which makes those narrow points much easier to handle, and we're always in favor of that!

Light and Shadow (4 blocks)

## Materials

*Yardages are based on 42"-wide fabrics. Fat eighths measure 9" x 21".*

1 fat eighth *each* of 112 assorted dark-background prints for blocks

1 fat eighth *each* of 56 assorted light-background prints for blocks

1¾ yards of lavender floral print for outer border and binding

⅜ yard of peach print for inner border

3¼ yards of fabric for backing

58" x 64" piece of batting

## Cutting

*All measurements include ¼"-wide seam allowances. Cut all strips across the width of the fabric (selvage to selvage) unless instructed otherwise.*

**From *each* of the 112 assorted dark-background prints, cut:**
2 rectangles, 2½" x 5" (224 total)

**From *each* of the 56 assorted light-background prints, cut:**
4 squares, 4½" x 4½" (224 total)

**From the peach print, cut:**
5 strips, 1½" x 42"

**From the *lengthwise grain* of the lavender floral print, cut:**
4 strips, 5" x 58½"
4 strips, 2" x 58½"

## TECHNIQUE TIP

When making a block with odd-shaped pieces, such as the two shapes in "Shadow Star," I make an extra copy of the block, and then, using a rotary cutter, cut out the two pieces on what would be the stitching line. I then use the paper template to "rough" cut the odd-shaped pieces, making sure to include at least a ¼" seam allowance on all sides of the template. You can follow the instructions for "Machine-Piecing Templates" on pages 10–11 to make a longer-lasting template, although in this situation you won't include the seam allowance.

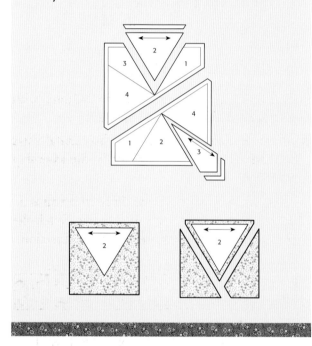

## *Making the Blocks*

For detailed instructions, refer to "Paper-Piecing Guidelines" on page 11. Use the 2½" x 5" rectangles for areas 1 and 3, and the 4½" x 4½" squares for areas 2 and 4.

1. Make 56 copies each of the foundation patterns on page 51. Trim the paper foundation ¼" from the outer (cutting) line.

2. Turn the foundation so that the blank (unmarked) side of the paper faces up. Position the fabric rectangle for piece 1, right side up, to cover area 1. Using the light from your sewing machine or another light source, look through the fabric and paper to make sure area 1 is completely covered, plus an ample seam allowance. Turn the paper and fabric over, being careful not to move the fabric, and pin the fabric in place through the marked side of the paper.

3. Once again, turn the foundation over to the unmarked side. Look through the paper and place a cut square of fabric for piece 2, right side up, over area 2. When fabric piece 2 is properly positioned, flip it on top of piece 1, right sides together.

4. Hold the layers in place, turn the foundation over, and carefully position the unit under the presser foot, paper side up. Sew on the line between areas 1 and 2, starting ¼" before the line and extending ¼" beyond.

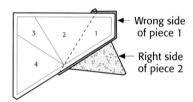

5. Remove the pin and open piece 2. Hold the block up to a light source and look through the fabric to be sure that the edges of piece 2 extend beyond the seam lines for area 2 on the foundation. Refold the fabrics and then fold the paper back to reveal the seam allowance. Place a ruler along the edge of the paper and trim the seam allowance to ¼".

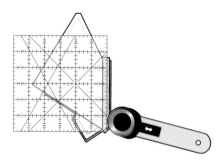

6. Open piece 2 and press the seam allowance to one side with a dry iron. Trim any excess fabric if necessary.

**7** Repeat steps 3–6 to add pieces 3 and 4. Make 56 scrappy unit As.

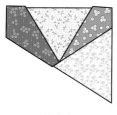

Unit A.
Make 56.

**8** Repeat steps 2–6 to make 56 scrappy unit Bs.

**9** Turn each unit paper side up. Align the ¼" line on your rotary ruler with the sewing line on the paper foundation. Use your rotary cutter to trim the foundation and fabrics ¼" from the sewing line on all sides.

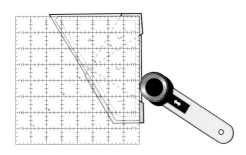

**10** Remove the paper foundation from each unit and sew a unit A and a unit B together as shown. Press the seams. You can reduce the bulk in the center of the block by pressing the seams in opposite directions. Refer to the technique tip on page 10, and gently position

both seam allowances as shown to distribute the fabric. Make 56 blocks.

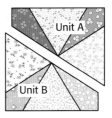

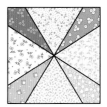

Unit A

Unit B

Make 56.

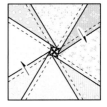

## Assembling the Quilt

For detailed instructions, refer to "Quilts with Blocks Set Side by Side" on page 12.

**1** Arrange the blocks into eight horizontal rows of seven blocks each as shown in the assembly diagram below.

**2** Sew the blocks into rows. Press the seams in alternate directions from row to row. Stitch the rows together. Press the seams in one direction.

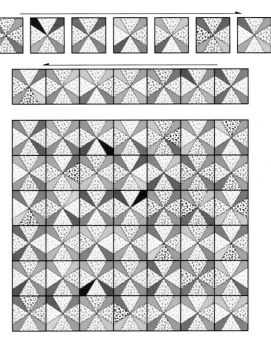

Assembly diagram

## Adding the Borders

For detailed instructions, refer to "Borders" on pages 13–14.

1. Join the 1½"-wide peach inner-border strips end to end to make a continuous strip. Measure the quilt through the center from top to bottom and cut two 1½"-wide inner-border strips from the long strip to fit that measurement.

2. Sew the cut inner-border strips to the side edges of the quilt top. Press toward the border strips.

3. Measure the quilt through the center from side to side, including the borders just added. Cut two 1½"-wide peach inner-border strips from the remainder of the long strip to fit that measurement.

4. Sew the cut inner-border strips to the top and bottom edges of the quilt top. Press toward the border strips.

5. Measure the quilt through the center from top to bottom and trim two 5"-wide lavender floral outer-border strips to fit that measurement.

6. Sew the trimmed outer-border strips to the side edges of the quilt top. Press toward the outer-border strips.

7. Measure the quilt through the center from side to side and trim the remaining 5"-wide lavender floral outer-border strips to fit that measurement.

8. Sew the trimmed outer-border strips to the top and bottom edges of the quilt top; press.

## Finishing the Quilt

For detailed instructions on the following finishing techniques, refer to "Finishing Your Quilt" on page 15.

1. Cut and piece the backing fabric so that it is 4" to 6" larger than the quilt top. Layer the quilt top with batting and backing. Baste the layers together.

2. Hand or machine quilt as desired. You may wish to quilt the borders and blocks in the ditch and add a teardrop design in the larger shape of each block. Finish by quilting a favorite continuous design in the border.

3. Square up the quilt sandwich.

4. Add a hanging sleeve, if desired.

5. Use the 2"-wide lavender floral strips for the binding. Sew the binding to the quilt. Add a label, if desired.

# DESIGN OPTIONS

If you find the number of fabrics required for "Shadow Star" a bit overwhelming, I've offered alternative designs below and on pages 48–50. Each design creates a different look: choose your favorite and have fun. I've included yardage requirements and how many pieces to cut from each fabric to make 56 blocks, the same number used in the quilt on page 42. Yardages for borders, backing, and binding, and measurements for batting, are the same as those listed on page 43.

## DESIGN A

This version is less scrappy than "Shadow Star" and only uses two color families. Be sure to choose distinctive groupings of light and dark fabrics or you'll lose your star points.

## Materials

1 fat quarter *each* of 24 assorted light-background prints: 12 with pink motifs and 12 with blue motifs

1 fat quarter *each* of 6 assorted blue prints

1 fat quarter *each* of 6 assorted pink prints

## Cutting

**From *each* light-background print, cut:**

3 strips, 4½" x 21"; crosscut into 10 squares, 4½" x 4½" (240 total). You'll have 16 squares left over. Set these aside for another project.

**From *each* assorted blue and pink print, cut:**

5 strips, 2½" x 21"; crosscut into 19 rectangles, 2½" x 5" (114 total of each color). You'll have 4 rectangles left over. Set these aside for another project.

# DESIGN B

In this design, the star points are scrappy but a cream solid is used throughout in place of background prints. This gives the design a lighter, brighter look.

## Materials

3⅝ yards of cream solid

⅜ yard *each* of 9 assorted pastel-background prints

## Cutting

**From the cream solid, cut:**
28 strips, 4½" x 42; crosscut into 224 squares, 4½" x 4½"

**From *each* pastel-background print, cut:**
4 strips, 2½" x 42"; crosscut into 25 rectangles, 2½" x 5". You'll have 1 rectangle left over. Set aside for another project.

# DESIGN C

Wonderful diagonal lines are created by the sharp contrast in values within this design. I've shown it with just two colors, each in two dark-background prints, and a cream background, but you could use multiple prints in each color; just make sure the value is the same in all the prints.

## Materials

3⅝ yards of cream solid

⅝ yard *each* of 4 dark-background prints

## Cutting

**From the cream solid, cut:**
28 strips, 4½" x 42"; crosscut into 224 squares, 4½" x 4½"

**From *each* dark-background print, cut:**
4 strips, 2½" x 42"; crosscut into 56 rectangles, 2½" x 5" (224 total)

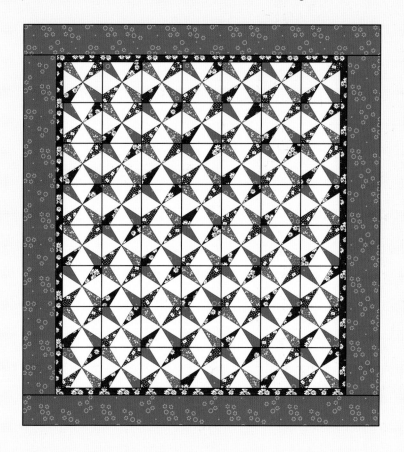

# DESIGN D

This option presents the traditional Light and Shadow pattern as printed in many publications. It is shown here in two solid fabrics, but the design would be sensational in any combination of two contrasting fabrics.

## Materials

3 yards of cream solid

3 yards of dark solid

## Cutting

**From the cream solid, cut:**

14 strips, 4½" x 42"; crosscut into 112 squares, 4½" x 4½"

14 strips, 2½" x 42"; crosscut into 112 rectangles, 2½" x 5"

**From the dark solid, cut:**

14 strips, 4½" x 42"; crosscut into 112 squares, 4½" x 4½"

14 strips, 2½" x 42"; crosscut into 112 rectangles, 2½" x 5"

**Unit A**

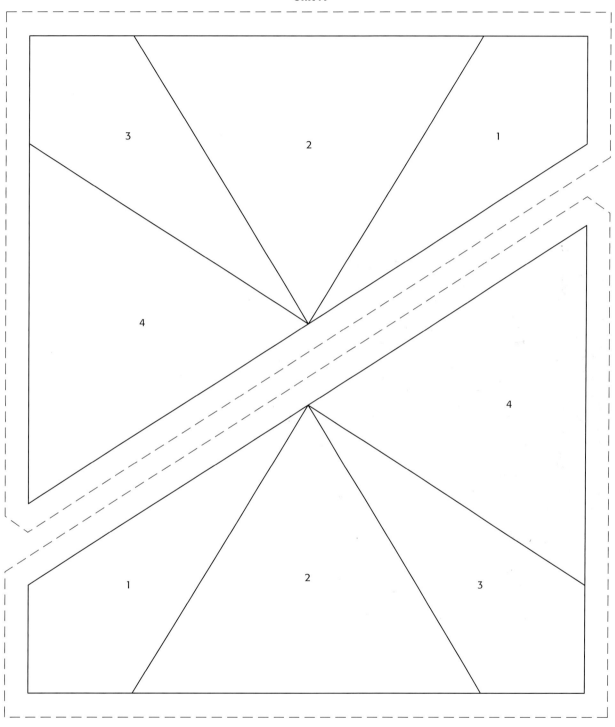

**Unit B**

# CHINESE CHECKERS

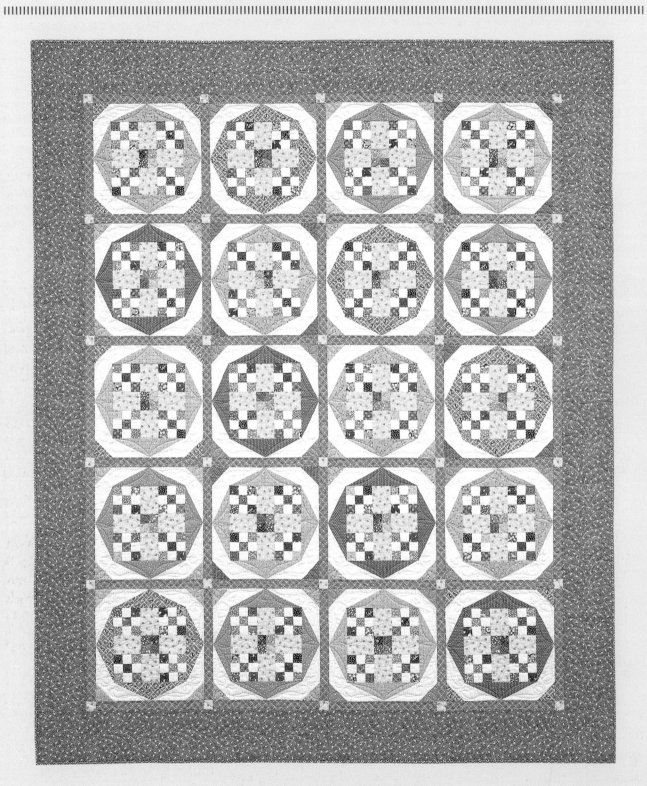

By Nancy Mahoney. Quilted by Dawn Kelly.
Finished Quilt Size: 64" x 77" • Finished Block Size: 12"

In a 1937 edition of the *Kansas City Star*, the Quilt without a Name pattern was described as "a lovely design. This quilt in dainty spring hues is an interesting piece of handwork." The original block was constructed using set-in seams and many odd-shaped pieces. I've revised the traditional design and updated the techniques, making the blocks easier to piece. With the addition of sashing, you don't need to worry about matching the block seams between the rows. Of course, that makes the sewing easier, too!

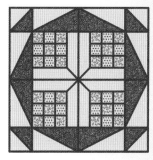

Quilt without a Name

## Materials

*Yardages are based on 42"-wide fabrics. Fat eighths measure 9" x 21".*

⅝ yard *each* of 5 assorted aqua prints for blocks

2⅞ yards of cream solid for blocks*

2 yards of pink-and-green print for border

⅞ yard of aqua plaid for sashing

¾ yard of yellow print for blocks and sashing

1 fat eighth *each* of 4 assorted blue prints for blocks

1 fat eighth *each* of 4 assorted pink prints for blocks

1 fat eighth *each* of 4 assorted lavender prints for blocks

1 fat eighth *each* of 4 assorted red prints for blocks

1 fat eighth *each* of 4 assorted peach and/or orange prints for blocks

⅝ yard of aqua floral print for binding

4½ yards of fabric for backing (vertical seam)

69" x 81" piece of batting

*\*If your fabric measures a true 42" after it has been washed and the selvages have been trimmed, you will only need 2¼ yards of this fabric.*

## Cutting

*All measurements include ¼"-wide seam allowances. Cut all strips across the width of the fabric (selvage to selvage) unless instructed otherwise. Template patterns for pieces A and B appear on page 57. For detailed instructions, refer to "Machine-Piecing Templates" on pages 10–11.*

**From the cream solid, cut:**
27 strips, 1½" x 21"

4 strips, 2⅞" x 42"; crosscut into 40 squares, 2⅞" x 2⅞"

160 pieces with template A

**Note: If you're using a solid fabric, you don't need to cut any reverse pieces; however, if your fabric has a right and wrong side, cut 80 pieces with template A and 80 pieces with template A reversed.**

**From the 4 assorted blue prints, cut a *total* of:**
9 strips, 1½" x 21"

**From *each* of the 4 assorted pink prints, cut:**
2 strips, 1½" x 21" (8 total)

**From *each* of the 4 assorted lavender prints, cut:**
2 strips, 1½" x 21" (8 total)

**From *each* of the 4 assorted red prints, cut:**
2 strips, 1½" x 21" (8 total)

From *each* of the 4 assorted peach and/or orange prints, cut:
2 strips, 1½" x 21" (8 total)

**From the yellow print, cut:**
5 strips, 3½" x 42"; crosscut into 80 rectangles, 2½" x 3½"

1 strip, 1½" x 42"

6 squares, 1½" x 1½"

**From *each* of the 5 assorted aqua prints, cut:**
1 strip, 2⅞" x 42"; crosscut into 8 squares, 2⅞" x 2⅞" (40 total)

16 pieces with template B (80 total)

**From the aqua plaid, cut:**
9 strips, 1½" x 42"; crosscut into 25 strips, 1½" x 12½"

1 strip, 12½" x 42"

**From the *lengthwise grain* of the pink-and-green print, cut:**
4 strips, 6" x 72"

**From the aqua floral print, cut:**
8 strips, 2" x 42"

---

## TECHNIQUE TIP

When you are tracing template patterns A and B, be sure to transfer the dots from the patterns onto the template material. Once you've cut out the templates, use a ⅛" hole-punch to make a small hole to mark each dot. As you trace the templates onto the fabric, place the point of a sharp pencil in the center of each hole to transfer the dots to fabric. Then, use a straight pin to match up and pin at the dots, add pins in between if needed, and sew the seam.

---

## *Making the Blocks*

For detailed instructions, refer to "Making Units from Strip Sets" on page 8 and "Half-Square-Triangle Units" on page 9.

**1** Sew one 1½" x 21" cream strip between two different 1½" x 21" assorted blue, pink, lavender, red, or peach and/or orange strips to make a strip set as shown; press. Make 13 scrappy strip sets and label them strip set A. Cut the strip sets into 1½"-wide segments. Cut 160 segments.

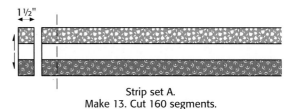

1½"

Strip set A.
Make 13. Cut 160 segments.

**2** Sew one 1½" x 21" assorted blue, pink, lavender, red, or peach and/or orange strip between two 1½" x 21" cream strips to make a strip set as shown; press. Make seven strip sets and label them strip set B. Cut the strip sets into 1½"-wide segments. Cut 80 segments.

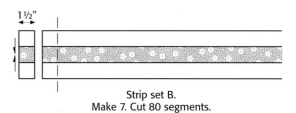

1½"

Strip set B.
Make 7. Cut 80 segments.

**3** Sew one segment from step 2 between two different segments from step 1 as shown; press. Make 80 scrappy nine-patch units.

Make 80.

**4** Sew two 1½" x 21" assorted blue, pink, lavender, red, or peach and/or orange strips together to make a strip set. Press toward the darker strip. Make four strip sets and label them strip set C. Cut the strip sets into 1½"-wide segments. Cut 40 segments.

1½"

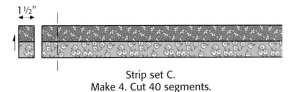

Strip set C.
Make 4. Cut 40 segments.

**5** Arrange and sew two random segments from step 4 as shown. Refer to the technique tip on page 10 for guidance on pressing the center seams. Make 20 scrappy four-patch units.

Make 20.

**6** Arrange four units from step 3, four 2½" x 3½" yellow rectangles, and one unit from step 5 as shown. Sew the units and rectangles in rows; press. Sew the rows together; press. Make 20.

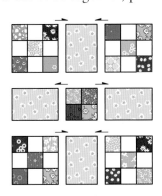

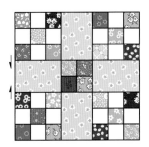

Make 20.

**7** Draw a diagonal line from corner to corner on the wrong side of each 2⅞" cream square. Place a marked square on a 2⅞" aqua square, right sides together, and stitch ¼" on each side of the marked diagonal line. Cut on the line to make two half-square-triangle units; press. Make 80 half-square-triangle units. Each unit should measure 2½" x 2½".

Make 80.

**8** Sew two cream A pieces (one regular and one reversed, if applicable) to adjacent sides of one assorted aqua B piece, as shown; press. Make 80 rectangle units.

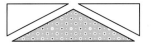

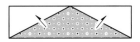

Make 80.

**9** Arrange four matching units from step 7, four matching units from step 8, and one unit from step 6 as shown. Sew the units together in rows; press. Sew the rows together; press. Make 20 blocks.

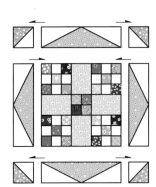 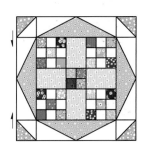

Make 20.

## Assembling the Quilt

For detailed instructions, refer to "Quilts with Sashing Units and Corner Squares" on page 12.

**1** Arrange and sew together five 1½" x 12½" aqua plaid sashing strips and four blocks, alternating them as shown to make a block row; press. Make five rows.

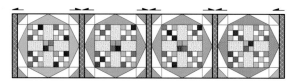

Make 5.

**2** Sew a 1½" x 42" yellow strip and a 12½" x 42" aqua plaid strip together to make a strip set; press. Cut the strip set into 1½"-wide segments. Cut 24 segments.

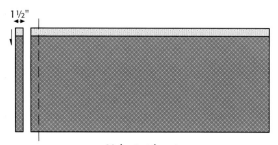

Make 1 strip set.
Cut 24 segments.

**3** Arrange and sew together four segments from step 2 and one 1½" yellow square as shown to make a sashing row; press. Make six rows.

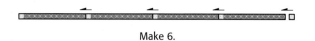

Make 6.

**4** Sew the block rows and sashing rows together, alternating them as shown in the assembly diagram below. Press the seams toward the sashing rows.

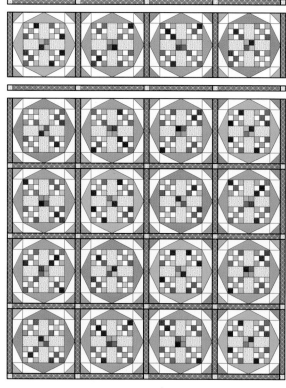

Assembly diagram

## Adding the Border

For detailed instructions, refer to "Borders" on pages 13–14.

**1** Measure the quilt through the center from top to bottom and trim two 6"-wide pink-and-green border strips to fit that measurement.

**2** Sew the trimmed border strips to the side edges of the quilt top. Press toward the border strips.

**3** Measure the quilt through the center from side to side, including the borders just added. Trim the remaining 6"-wide pink-and-green border strips to fit that measurement.

**4** Sew the trimmed border strips to the top and bottom edges of the quilt top; press.

## Finishing the Quilt

For detailed instructions on the following finishing techniques, refer to "Finishing Your Quilt" on page 15.

**1** Cut and piece the backing fabric so that it is 4" to 6" larger than the quilt top. Layer the quilt top with batting and backing (vertical seam). Baste the layers together.

**2** Hand or machine quilt as desired. You may wish to quilt swags, swirls, and ovals in each block, and small loops in the sashing. Finish by quilting a feather design in the border.

**3** Square up the quilt sandwich.

**4** Add a hanging sleeve, if desired.

**5** Use the 2"-wide aqua floral strips to make the binding. Sew the binding to the quilt. Add a label, if desired.

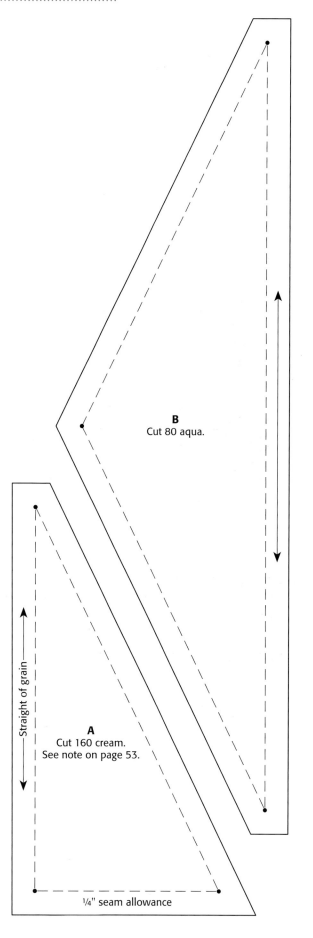

**B**
Cut 80 aqua.

Straight of grain

**A**
Cut 160 cream.
See note on page 53.

¼" seam allowance

# PATRIOTIC STAR

By Nancy Mahoney. Quilted by Dawn Kelly.

Finished Quilt Size: 57" x 72"  •  Finished Block Size: 14"

The appearance of "Patriotic Star" can be greatly altered by how you position the colors, which is what makes playing with fabric so much fun! This design, published in the *Kansas City Star* in 1936, was contributed by a reader. The newspaper described it as a lovely pattern and a good design for using up your scraps of red, white, and blue material. The red-and-blue stars set on the cream solid are particularly dramatic and lend a patriotic, Independence Day touch to this quilt. Nevertheless, you'll want to use it throughout the year, not just for the holiday.

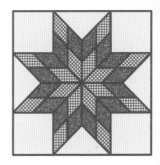

Patriotic Star

# Materials

*Yardages are based on 42"-wide fabrics.*

¼ yard *each* of 6 assorted blue prints for blocks

¼ yard *each* of 6 assorted light-background prints for blocks

⅜ yard *each* of 6 assorted red prints for blocks

2 yards of dark blue print for sashing, outer border, and binding

1⅝ yards of cream solid for blocks

¾ yard of red print for sashing and inner border

3½ yards of fabric for backing

61" x 77" piece of batting

# Cutting

*All measurements include ¼"-wide seam allowances. Cut all strips across the width of the fabric (selvage to selvage) unless instructed otherwise.*

From *each* of the 6 assorted blue prints, cut:
2 strips, 2" x 24" (12 total)

From *each* of the 6 assorted red prints, cut:
4 strips, 2" x 24" (24 total)

From *each* of the 6 assorted light-background prints, cut:
2 strips, 2" x 24" (12 total)

From the cream solid, cut:
6 strips, 5" x 42", crosscut into 48 squares, 5" x 5"

3 strips, 7½" x 42"; crosscut into 12 squares, 7½" x 7½". Cut each square twice diagonally to yield 48 quarter-square triangles.

From the red print for sashing and inner border, cut:
9 strips, 1½" x 42"; crosscut into 17 strips, 1½" x 14½"

6 strips, 1½" x 42"

From the *lengthwise grain* of the dark blue print, cut:
6 squares, 1½" x 1½"

4 strips, 6" x 67"

4 strips, 2" x 67"

## *Making the Blocks*

For detailed instructions, refer to "Making Units from Strip Sets" on page 8.

**1** Sew a 2" x 24" assorted blue strip and a 2" x 24" assorted red strip together, offsetting the strips by 2" as shown, to make strip set A. Press the seam open. Make 12 of strip set A in matching sets of two. Position your ruler so that the 45° diagonal marking is aligned with the seam line, and trim the left end of each strip set as shown.

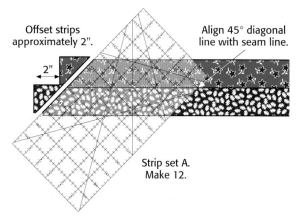

Offset strips approximately 2".

Align 45° diagonal line with seam line.

2"

Strip set A.
Make 12.

**2** Position your ruler so that the 45° diagonal marking aligns with the seam line and the 2" measurement is even with the angled edge of the strip set as shown. Cut eight 2"-wide segments from each strip set (96 total).

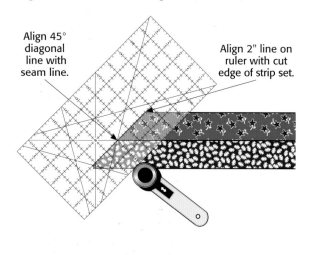

Align 45° diagonal line with seam line.

Align 2" line on ruler with cut edge of strip set.

Cut 8 segments from each strip set (96 total).

**3** Repeat steps 1 and 2, using a 2" x 24" assorted light-background strip and a 2" x 24" assorted red strip to make strip set B; press. Make 12 of strip set B. Cut eight 2"-wide segments from each strip set (96 total).

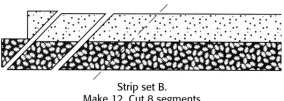

Strip set B.
Make 12. Cut 8 segments from each strip set (96 total).

**4** To make one block, place one segment from step 2 on top of one segment with matching red fabric from step 3, right sides together. Offset the point at the top edge ¼" as shown. Sew the segments together. Press the seam open. Make eight matching diamond units.

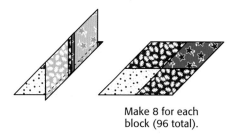

Make 8 for each block (96 total).

**5** On the wrong side of each unit or piece and as shown below, mark opposite corners of all diamond units from step 4, one corner of four 5" cream squares, and the right-angle corner of four cream triangles ¼" from the raw edge in preparation for Y-seam construction. Note that the squares and triangles have been cut slightly oversized and will be trimmed after the block is pieced.

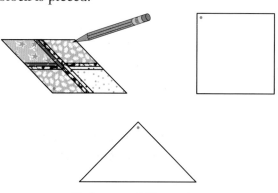

Mark corners ¼" from edge.

6 Arrange two diamond units and one marked cream triangle as shown. Place the cream triangle on top of the diamond unit, right sides together. Align the raw edges, matching the ¼" mark on the cream triangle to the ¼" mark on the diamond unit beneath it. Starting with a backstitch at the ¼" mark, sew to the outside raw edge. Press toward the triangle.

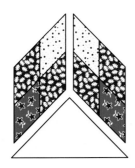

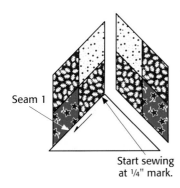

Seam 1

Start sewing at ¼" mark.

7 With right sides together, position the second diamond unit on top of the unit from step 6. Align the raw edges and match the ¼" marks. Starting with a backstitch at the ¼" mark, sew to the outside raw edge. Press toward the triangle.

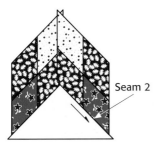

Seam 2

8 Place the two diamond units right sides together, and with raw edges and seam lines

aligned. Starting with a small backstitch at the ¼" mark, sew to the diamond tip. Press the seams open.

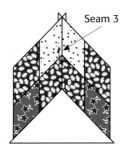

Seam 3

9 Repeat steps 6–8 to make a total of four identical diamond units with Y seams.

10 Arrange two diamond units from step 9 and a marked 5" cream square as shown. Place the cream square on top of one diamond unit, right sides together. Align the raw edges, matching the ¼" mark on the cream square to the ¼" mark on the diamond unit beneath it. Starting with a small backstitch at the ¼" mark, sew to the outside edge. Press toward the square.

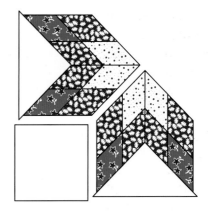

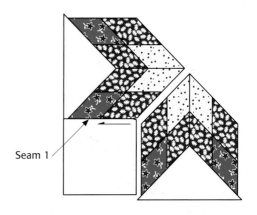

Seam 1

**11** With right sides together, position the second diamond unit on top of the unit from step 10. Align the raw edges and match the ¼" marks. Starting with a small backstitch at the ¼" mark, sew to the outside raw edge. Press toward the square.

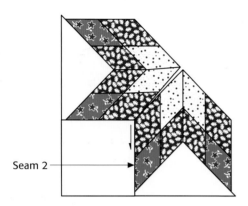

**12** Place the two diamond units right sides together, and with raw edges and seam lines aligned. Starting with a small backstitch at the ¼" mark, sew to the diamond tip. Press the seams open.

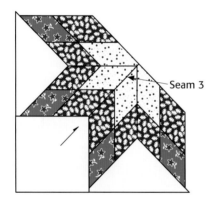

**13** With right sides together, position a marked 5" cream square on top of one diamond unit from step 12 as shown. Align the raw edges and match the ¼" marks. Starting with a small backstitch at the ¼" mark, sew to the outside raw edge. Press toward the square.

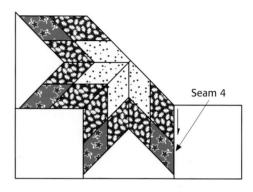

**14** Repeat steps 10–13 to make a second half-block unit.

**15** Place the two half-block units from steps 13 and 14 right sides together with a diamond unit on top of a corner square. Align the raw edges and match the ¼" marks. Starting with a small backstitch, sew seam 1 to the outside edges. Press toward the square. Flip the half-block units over so that a diamond unit is on top of the opposite corner square. Starting with a small backstitch, sew seam 2; press.

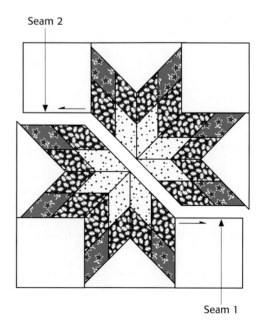

16 Keeping the half-block units right sides together, align and pin the star-center seam intersections and the seams in between. Sew the center seam, starting and stopping at the ¼" marks with a small backstitch. Press the seam open.

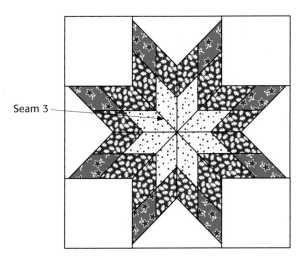

Seam 3

17 Repeat steps 4–16 to make a total of 12 blocks. Each block should measure 14½" x 14½" (including seam allowance). To trim and/or straighten the edges of each block, align the ¼" mark on your ruler with the star points. Use a rotary cutter to trim any excess fabric ¼" from the star points, leaving a ¼" seam allowance for joining the blocks. Square the corners of the blocks as necessary.

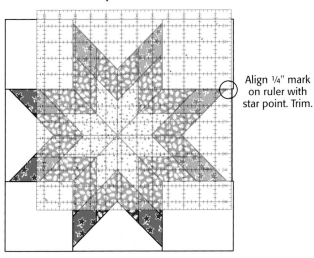

Align ¼" mark on ruler with star point. Trim.

Make 12 blocks.

## Assembling the Quilt

For detailed instructions, refer to "Quilts with Sashing Units and Corner Squares" on page 12.

1 Arrange and sew together three blocks and two 1½" x 14½" red sashing strips, alternating them as shown to make a block row; press. Make four rows.

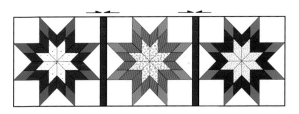

Make 4.

2 Sew together three 1½" x 14½" red sashing strips and two 1½" dark blue squares as shown to make a sashing row; press. Make three rows.

Make 3.

**3** Sew the block rows and sashing rows together, alternating them as shown in the assembly diagram below. Press the seams toward the sashing rows.

Assembly diagram

## Adding the Borders

For detailed instructions, refer to "Borders" on pages 13–14.

**1** Join the 1½"-wide red inner-border strips end to end to make a continuous strip. Measure the quilt through the center from top to bottom and cut two 1½"-wide inner-border strips from the long strip to fit that measurement.

**2** Sew the cut inner-border strips to the side edges of the quilt top. Press toward the border strips.

**3** Measure the quilt through the center from side to side, including the borders just added. Cut two 1½"-wide red inner-border strips from the remainder of the long strip to fit that measurement.

**4** Sew the cut inner-border strips to the top and bottom edges of the quilt top. Press toward the border strips.

**5** Measure the quilt through the center from top to bottom and trim two 6"-wide dark blue outer-border strips to fit that measurement.

**6** Sew the trimmed outer-border strips to the side edges of the quilt. Press toward the outer-border strips.

**7** Measure the quilt through the center from side to side and trim the remaining 6"-wide dark blue outer-border strips to fit that measurement.

**8** Sew the trimmed outer-border strips to the top and bottom edges of the quilt; press.

## Finishing the Quilt

For detailed instructions on the following finishing techniques, refer to "Finishing Your Quilt" on page 15.

1. Cut and piece the backing fabric so that it is 4" to 6" larger than the quilt top. Layer the quilt top with batting and backing. Baste the layers together.

2. Hand or machine quilt as desired. You may wish to quilt curved lines and swags in the blocks. Finish by quilting a feather design in the outer border.

3. Square up the quilt sandwich.

4. Add a hanging sleeve, if desired.

5. Use the 2"-wide dark blue strips to make the binding. Sew the binding to the quilt. Add a label, if desired.

# PEPPERMINT TWIST

By Nancy Mahoney

Finished Quilt Size: 48½" x 54½"  •  Finished Block Size: 3"

The Ozark Tile pattern is an allover quilt pattern. When printed in a 1937 newspaper, the design combined solid squares of one color with blocks of varied prints. I've updated the design, making it a breeze to stitch using only squares. This small quilt is so quick and easy, it will zoom together in no time.

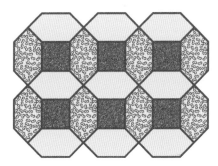

Ozark Tile

## Materials

*Yardages are based on 42"-wide fabrics. Fat quarters measure 18" x 21" and fat eighths measure 9" x 21".*

1⅝ yards of pink floral print for outer border and binding

1 fat quarter *each* of 5 assorted pink prints for blocks

1 fat eighth *each* of 3 assorted pink prints for blocks

1 fat eighth *each* of 8 assorted blue prints for blocks

⅞ yard of light-background print for blocks

⅜ yard of light blue print for inner border

3 yards of fabric for backing

52" x 58" piece of batting

## Cutting

*All measurements include ¼"-wide seam allowances. Cut all strips across the width of the fabric (selvage to selvage) unless instructed otherwise.*

**From the light-background print, cut:**
3 strips, 4¼" x 42"; crosscut into 25 squares, 4¼" x 4¼"

4 strips, 3½" x 42"; crosscut into 42 squares, 3½" x 3½"

**From *each* of the 5 fat quarters of assorted pink prints, cut:**
5 squares, 4¼" x 4¼" (25 total)

7 squares, 3½" x 3½" (35 total)

**From *each* of the 3 fat eighths of assorted pink prints, cut:**
7 squares, 3½" x 3½" (21 total)

**From *each* of the 8 assorted blue prints, cut:**
6 squares, 3½" x 3½" (48 total)

**From the light blue print, cut:**
5 strips, 1¼" x 42"

**From the *lengthwise grain* of the pink floral print, cut:**
4 strips, 4½" x 54"

4 strips, 2" x 54"

## Making the Blocks

For detailed instructions, refer to "Half-Square-Triangle Units" on page 9.

① Draw a diagonal line from corner to corner on the wrong side of each 4¼" light-background square. Place a marked square on a 4¼" assorted pink square, right sides together, and stitch ¼" on each side of the marked diagonal line. Cut on the line to make two half-square-triangle units; press. You will make 50 half-square-triangle units. Each unit should measure 3⅞" x 3⅞".

Make 50.

② Layer two half-square triangle units from step 1 right sides together so that the pink fabric covers the light fabric and the seam allowances nestle next to each other. Draw a diagonal line from corner to corner on the top unit in the opposite direction from the seam. Stitch ¼" on each side of the new diagonal line and cut on the marked line to make two hourglass units. Referring to the technique tip on page 10, gently position both seam allowances and press each new unit. Make 49 hourglass units. You'll have one unit left over. Set this aside for another project. Each unit should measure 3½" x 3½".

Make 49.

## Assembling the Quilt

For detailed instructions, refer to "Quilts with Blocks Set Side by Side" on page 12.

① Arrange seven 3½" assorted pink squares and six 3½" assorted blue squares, alternating them as shown. Sew the squares together; press. Make eight rows.

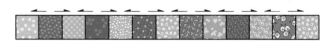

Make 8.

② Arrange seven hourglass units and six 3½" light-background squares, alternating them as shown. Sew the units and squares together; press. Make seven rows.

Make 7.

③ Arrange and sew the rows from steps 1 and 2 together, alternating them as shown in the assembly diagram below. Press the seams away from the hourglass rows.

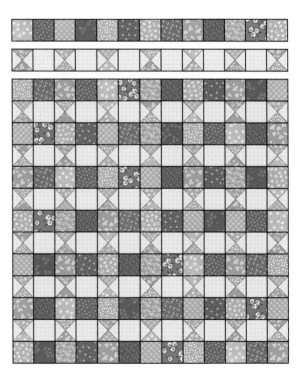

Assembly diagram

## Adding the Borders

For detailed instructions, refer to "Borders" on pages 13–14.

1. Join the 1¼"-wide light blue inner-border strips end to end to make a continuous strip. Measure the quilt through the center from top to bottom and cut two 1¼"-wide inner-border strips from the long strip to fit that measurement.

2. Sew the cut inner-border strips to the side edges of the quilt top. Press toward the border strips.

3. Measure the quilt through the center from side to side, including the borders just added. Cut two 1¼"-wide light blue inner-border strips from the remainder of the long strip to fit that measurement.

4. Sew the cut inner-border strips to the top and bottom edges of the quilt top. Press toward the border strips.

5. Measure the quilt through the center from top to bottom and trim two 4½"-wide pink floral outer-border strips to fit that measurement.

6. Sew the trimmed outer-border strips to the side edges of the quilt. Press toward the outer-border strips.

7. Measure the quilt through the center from side to side and trim the remaining 4½"-wide pink floral outer-border strips to fit that measurement.

8. Sew the trimmed outer-border strips to the top and bottom edges of the quilt; press.

## Finishing the Quilt

For detailed instructions on the following finishing techniques, refer to "Finishing Your Quilt" on page 15.

1. Cut and piece the backing fabric so that it is 4" to 6" larger than the quilt top. Layer the quilt top with batting and backing. Baste the layers together.

2. Hand or machine quilt as desired. You may wish to quilt the borders and squares in the ditch and add an oval medallion design. Finish by quilting a favorite continuous design in the border.

3. Square up the quilt sandwich.

4. Add a hanging sleeve, if desired.

5. Use the 2"-wide pink floral strips to make the binding. Sew the binding to the quilt. Add a label, if desired.

6
4

114   2½ x 8½

# $\mathscr{F}$LYING $\mathscr{K}$ITES

||||||||||||||||||||||||||||||||||||||||||||||||||||||||||||||||||||||||||

By Nancy Mahoney

Finished Quilt Size: 52" x 62"  •  Finished Block Size: 8"

|||||||||

This simple and effective quilt pattern was contributed to the *Kansas City Star* by a reader in 1937. The newspaper described the pattern as "a Flying Kite for porch work sewing." In this quilt, the wide yellow sashing has a calming effect on the spinning pinwheels and makes the sewing easier, too. The addition of the darker blue outer border is the crowning touch to this perky quilt.

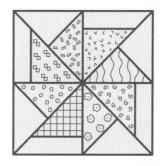

Flying Kite

## Materials

*Yardages are based on 42"-wide fabrics. Fat eighths measure 9" x 21".*

1⅞ yards of dark blue floral print for border and binding

1⅛ yards of yellow solid for sashing

1⅛ yards of cream solid for blocks and sashing squares

1 fat eighth *each* of 4 assorted pink prints for blocks

1 fat eighth *each* of 4 assorted blue prints for blocks

1 fat eighth *each* of 4 assorted green prints for blocks

1 fat eighth *each* of 4 assorted lavender prints for blocks

1 fat eighth *each* of 4 assorted yellow prints for blocks

3⅛ yards of fabric for backing

56" x 66" piece of batting

## Cutting

*All measurements include ¼"-wide seam allowances. Cut all strips across the width of the fabric (selvage to selvage) unless instructed otherwise.*

**From the cream solid, cut:**

3 strips, 5¼" x 42"; crosscut into 20 squares, 5¼" x 5¼". Cut each square twice diagonally to yield 80 quarter-square triangles.

10 strips, 1½" x 42"; crosscut into 80 rectangles, 1½" x 4⅞"

2 strips, 2½" x 42", crosscut into 30 squares, 2½" x 2½"

**From *each* of the 4 assorted pink prints, cut:**

1 square, 5¼" x 5¼"; crosscut twice diagonally to yield 4 quarter-square triangles (16 total)

2 squares, 3⅞" x 3⅞"; crosscut once diagonally to yield 4 half-square triangles (16 total)

**From *each* of the 4 assorted blue prints, cut:**

1 square, 5¼" x 5¼"; crosscut twice diagonally to yield 4 quarter-square triangles (16 total)

2 squares, 3⅞" x 3⅞"; crosscut once diagonally to yield 4 half-square triangles (16 total)

From *each* of the 4 assorted green prints, cut:

1 square, 5¼" x 5¼"; crosscut twice diagonally to yield 4 quarter-square triangles (16 total)

2 squares, 3⅞" x 3⅞"; crosscut once diagonally to yield 4 half-square triangles (16 total)

From *each* of the 4 assorted lavender prints, cut:

1 square, 5¼" x 5¼"; crosscut twice diagonally to yield 4 quarter-square triangles (16 total)

2 squares, 3⅞" x 3⅞"; crosscut once diagonally to yield 4 half-square triangles (16 total)

From *each* of the 4 assorted yellow prints, cut:

1 square, 5¼" x 5¼"; crosscut twice diagonally to yield 4 quarter-square triangles (16 total)

2 squares, 3⅞" x 3⅞"; crosscut once diagonally to yield 4 half-square triangles (16 total)

From the yellow solid, cut:

13 strips, 2½" x 42"; crosscut into 49 strips, 2½" x 8½"

From the *lengthwise grain* of the dark blue floral print, cut:

4 strips, 5½" x 58"

5 strips, 2" x 58"

## Making the Blocks

1 Arrange and sew a 5¼" cream triangle and a 5¼" assorted pink, blue, green, lavender, or yellow triangle as shown in the tip box at right; press. Make 80.

### TECHNIQUE TIP

Make one stack of cream triangles and a second stack of assorted print triangles. Position the stacks of triangles as shown. This will prevent you from sewing the triangles together the wrong way.

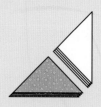 

Make 80.

2 Sew a 1½" x 4⅞" cream rectangle and a 3⅞" assorted pink, blue, green, lavender, or yellow triangle together as shown; press. Position your ruler so that the 45° diagonal marking is aligned with the straight outside edge of the unit, and the edge of the ruler is aligned with the corner and the diagonal edge of the unit. Trim the excess fabric as shown. Make 80.

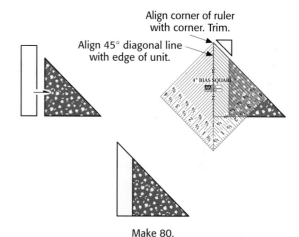

Align corner of ruler with corner. Trim.

Align 45° diagonal line with edge of unit.

Make 80.

**Note: At this point, you may find it helpful to sort the units into color-matched sets of four for each block.**

**❸** Arrange and sew a unit from step 1 and a unit from step 2 as shown; press. Make 80 in color-matched sets of four.

Make 80.

**❹** Arrange four color-matched units from step 3 as shown. Sew the units in rows; press. Sew the rows together, carefully matching the intersecting center seams. Refer to the technique tip on page 10 for guidance on positioning and pressing the center seam allowances. Make 20 blocks.

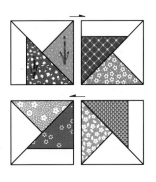

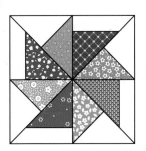

Make 20.

## TECHNIQUE TIP

If you prefer, use the shortcut technique for making half-square-triangle units described on page 9; then cut the half-square-triangle units to make the quarter-square-triangle units shown below. Since you will use only one half of each unit in this quilt, you'll need to make twice as many units, but you'll have enough left over to make another quilt with the pinwheel kites turning in the opposite direction. As an alternative, you can make the same number of units and combine both blocks in the same quilt.

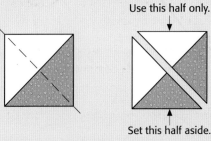

Use this half only.

Set this half aside.

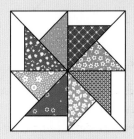

Clockwise pinwheels

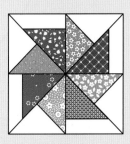

Counter-clockwise pinwheels

## Assembling the Quilt

For detailed instructions, refer to "Quilts with Sashing Units and Corner Squares" on page 12.

**1** Arrange and sew together five 2½" x 8½" yellow solid sashing strips and four blocks, alternating them as shown to make a block row; press. Make five rows.

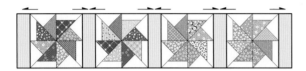

Make 5.

**2** Arrange and sew together five 2½" cream squares and four 2½" x 8½" yellow sashing strips, alternating them as shown to make a sashing row; press. Make six rows.

Make 6.

**3** Sew the block rows and sashing rows together, alternating them as shown in the assembly diagram below. Press the seams toward the sashing rows.

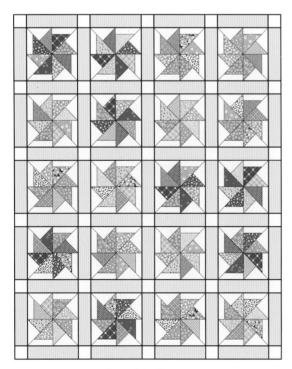

Assembly diagram

## Adding the Border

For detailed instructions, refer to "Borders" on pages 13–14.

**1** Measure the quilt through the center from top to bottom and trim two 5½"-wide dark blue floral border strips to fit that measurement.

**2** Sew the trimmed border strips to the side edges of the quilt top. Press toward the border strips.

**3** Measure the quilt through the center from side to side, including the borders just added. Trim the remaining 5½"-wide dark blue floral border strips to fit that measurement.

**4** Sew the trimmed border strips to the top and bottom edges of the quilt top; press.

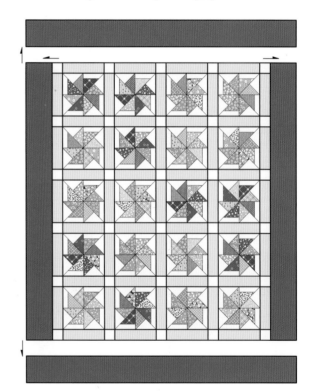

## *Finishing the Quilt*

For detailed instructions on the following finishing techniques, refer to "Finishing Your Quilt" on page 15.

**1** Cut and piece the backing fabric so that it is 4" to 6" larger than the quilt top. Layer the quilt top with batting and backing. Baste the layers together.

**2** Hand or machine quilt as desired. You may wish to quilt each block in the ditch, with a curved design in the block center, and the sashing in the ditch with small loops running down the center of each sash. Finish by quilting leaves and loops in the border.

**3** Square up the quilt sandwich.

**4** Add a hanging sleeve, if desired.

**5** Use the 2"-wide dark blue floral strips to make the binding. Sew the binding to the quilt. Add a label, if desired.

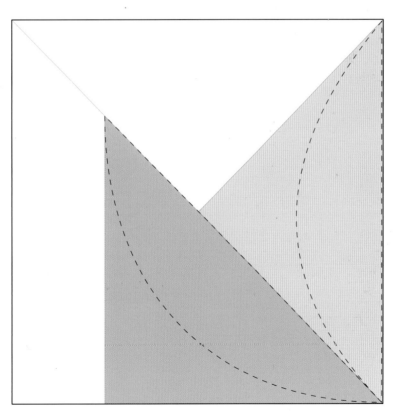

Pinwheel quilting motif

# RED MAGNOLIAS

By Nancy Mahoney

Finished Quilt Size: 45¼" x 45¼" • Finished Block Size: 9"

In 1934, the *San Antonio Light* wrote, "When a quiltmaker is looking for a quilt that is so lovely in design that she will be proud to claim it as her handi-work, and yet at the same time wants a pattern that is very simple to do, she selects the Magnolia. Not only is the pattern an easy one to cut, but it is a very simple block to make." The red-and-green color scheme makes this charming quilt perfect for holiday decorating, or—with slight alterations to the palette—to celebrate spring.

Magnolia

## Materials

*Yardages are based on 42"-wide fabrics. Fat eighths measure 9" x 21".*

1⅝ yards of cream solid for blocks and setting triangles

1⅝ yards of red check for border and binding

1 fat eighth *each* of 9 assorted red prints for blocks

½ yard of green print for blocks

3 yards of fabric for backing

50" x 50" piece of batting

## Cutting

*All measurements include ¼"-wide seam allowances. Cut all strips across the width of the fabric (selvage to selvage) unless instructed otherwise.*

**From the cream solid, cut:**
8 strips, 2" x 42"; crosscut into 78 rectangles, 2" x 3½"

2 strips, 2" x 42"; crosscut into 26 squares, 2" x 2"

2 strips, 3⅞" x 42"; crosscut into 13 squares, 3⅞" x 3⅞". Cut once diagonally to yield 26 half-square triangles.

2 squares, 14½" x 14½"; cut twice diagonally to yield 8 quarter-square triangles

2 squares, 7½" x 7½"; cut once diagonally to yield 4 half-square triangles

**From *each* of the 9 assorted red prints, cut:**
3 rectangles, 2" x 3½" (27 total); you'll have 1 rectangle left over

3 rectangles, 2" x 5" (27 total); you'll have 1 rectangle left over

3 rectangles, 2" x 6½" (27 total); you'll have 1 rectangle left over

**From the green print, cut:**
7 strips, 2" x 42"; crosscut into 26 rectangles, 2" x 9⅞"

**From the *lengthwise grain* of the red check, cut:**
4 strips, 4" x 49"

4 strips, 2" x 49"

## Making the Blocks

For detailed instructions, refer to "Cut Corners" on pages 9–10.

❶ Place a 2" x 3½" cream rectangle on one end of a 2" x 3½" assorted red rectangle, right sides together, as shown. Draw a diagonal line on the wrong side of the cream rectangle as shown. Stitch on the marked diagonal line. Trim ¼" from the stitching line; press. Make 13 of each.

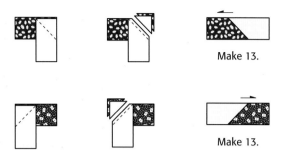

Make 13.

Make 13.

**2** Repeat step 1 using 2" x 3½" cream rectangles and 2" x 5" assorted red rectangles as shown. Make 13 of each.

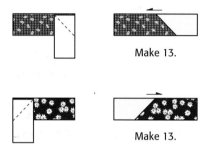

Make 13.

Make 13.

**3** Repeat step 1 using 2" x 3½" cream rectangles and 2" x 6½" assorted red rectangles as shown. Make 13 of each.

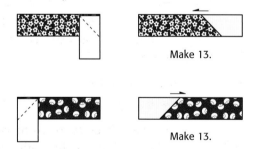

Make 13.

Make 13.

**4** Repeat step 1 using 2" cream squares and 2" x 9⅞" green rectangles as shown. Make 13 of each.

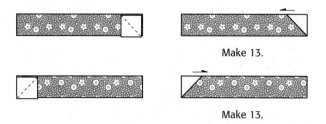

Make 13.

Make 13.

**5** Arrange one of each unit and reverse unit from steps 1–4 and two 3⅞" cream triangles as shown. Sew the pieces together to make a half block and a reverse half block; press. Make 13 of each.

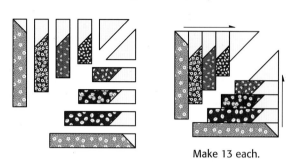

Make 13 each.

**6** Position your ruler so that the 45° diagonal marking is aligned with a seam line, and the edge of the ruler is even with the diagonal edge and the corner of a half block from step 5. Trim and straighten the staggered edge of the unit as shown. Repeat to trim all step 5 half blocks, both regular and reverse.

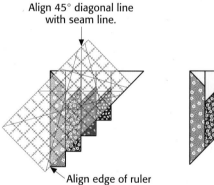

Align 45° diagonal line with seam line.

Align edge of ruler with corner. Trim.

**7** Sew a half block and a reverse half block from step 6 together as shown; press. Make 13 scrappy blocks.

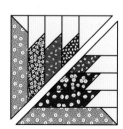
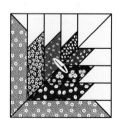

Make 13.

## Assembling the Quilt

For detailed instructions, refer to "Quilts Set Diagonally" on page 13. The setting triangles have been cut oversized. You will trim them after the quilt center is assembled.

❶ Arrange the blocks in diagonal rows as shown in the assembly diagram below. Add the cream quarter-square side setting triangles.

❷ Sew the blocks and side triangles together in rows; press.

❸ Sew the rows together, adding the cream half-square corner setting triangles last. Press the seams toward the cream triangles.

❹ To trim and straighten the quilt top, align the ¼" mark on your ruler with the outermost points of the blocks. Use a rotary cutter to trim any excess fabric, leaving a ¼"-wide seam allowance for adding the border. Square the corners of the quilt top as necessary.

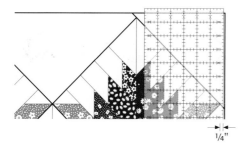

1/4"

## Adding the Border

For detailed instructions, refer to "Borders" on pages 13–14.

❶ Measure the quilt through the center from top to bottom and trim two 4"-wide red check border strips to fit that measurement.

❷ Sew the trimmed border strips to the side edges of the quilt top. Press toward the border strips.

❸ Measure the quilt through the center from side to side, including the borders just added. Trim the remaining 4"-wide red check border strips to fit that measurement.

❹ Sew the trimmed border strips to the top and bottom edges of the quilt top; press.

## Finishing the Quilt

For detailed instructions on the following finishing techniques, refer to "Finishing Your Quilt" on page 15.

❶ Cut and piece the backing fabric so that it is 4" to 6" larger than the quilt top. Layer the quilt top with batting and backing. Baste the layers together.

❷ Hand or machine quilt as desired. You may wish to quilt each block in the ditch, with a medallion design in the center, and a partial medallion in the side and corner setting triangles. Finish by quilting a favorite continuous design in the border.

❸ Square up the quilt sandwich.

❹ Add a hanging sleeve, if desired.

❺ Use the 2"-wide red check strips to make the binding. Sew the binding to the quilt. Add a label, if desired.

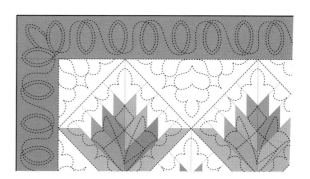

# ABOUT THE AUTHOR

Author, teacher, fabric designer, and award-winning quiltmaker, Nancy Mahoney has enjoyed making quilts for more than 20 years. An impressive range of her beautiful quilts have been featured in many books and national quilt magazines.

*Quilt Revival* is Nancy's sixth book with Martingale & Company. Her other bestselling books include *Patchwork Showcase* (2004), *Basket Bonanza* (2005), and *Quilt Block Bonanza: 50 Paper-Pieced Designs* (2005).

Almost entirely self-taught, Nancy continues to explore new ways to combine traditional blocks and updated techniques to create quilts that are easy to make.

Nancy lives in Palm Coast, Florida, with her life partner of 30 years, Tom, and their umbrella cockatoo, Prince.